A Walk in Rose's Garden

Our Stepping Stones in Life

KAREN SWASEY

Edited by Lil Barcaski and Linda Hinkle

Published by: GWN Publishing
www.GWNPublishing.com

Cover Design: Kristina Conatser

ISBN: 978-1-959608-55-4

DEDICATION

In memory of those who have found their angel wings,
may you be always remembered.

Through all our memories let us preserve our heritage
for our children's children; in honor of a life lived.

CONTENTS

The lives of the people whose stories I will share with you in this book will take you through a pathway of their transitions in life. Journey with us through Rose's Garden as we reflect upon the steppingstones of one's life and honor their journey. Embrace the memories and honor their story.

In honor of all those who walk through the pathway of life to the light on the other side.

CHAPTER 1

REFLECTIONS OF THE SOUL

*"People with a teachable spirit approach each
day as an opportunity for another learning
experience."*

T hese words are shared by John C. Maxwell, and they
have become a daily prayer that I repeat at the beginning of each day. Give me a *teachable spirit* and an
open heart. This is an intentional act of being alert, on
the lookout for "something new" while knowing that success has
less to do with possessing natural talent, but more to do with
choosing to learn from each encounter.

A Walk in Rose's Garden is encompassed within our tapestry of
life, as it is the path of life's reflection. Rose's garden consists of
all the emotions that people experience throughout their lifetime. We used this program in the communities that I managed,
and we intentionally based their care to include the experiences
of a person's journey, or as we say, their path in life. We found
how important it was, as you may have read in my book, *The
Runner Who Never Ran: A Game Warden's Daughter*, where I

share how our narrative story is essential in honoring the life that we have journeyed. By looking at the reflections of the soul, we can honor each path that one may have gone down. Whether it is their profession, their family life, their childhood, or even their dreams, we always made sure that we focused on this as a priority as it is the true reflection of our soul.

In one of our buildings, we focused *A Walk in Rose's Garden* around a hospice program. This program was created based on a person by the name of Rose who had a gentle spirit and had a vivacious view on life. She embraced all the gifts she received throughout her lifetime, and she always took the time to stop and enjoy the simplest things in life. She embodied that teachable spirit of taking the moment to sit and truly look at the gifts that God has given us. Her garden was her spirit in life. She never wanted to miss an opportunity to learn, and in turn, to experience life's journey. She taught us the importance of a narrative story, or narrative medicine. Narrative medicine is something that we practiced in a care model called, the Grace Model of Care. We would concentrate on people's life stories and see how they might reflect upon their illness. Sometimes it would show the social challenges they faced or labeled by being diagnosed with a disease or deformity. This labeling can sometimes create outcomes such as depression, being angry with life, and even isolation tendencies. Narrative medicine is a known medical approach as a commitment of understanding the person's life, and then using this knowledge in the story. This meant looking at life through their lenses, with an intent of understanding what it was like to walk in their shoes.

Thinking about the act of labeling somebody brings back memories from my childhood. Well, you see, there was a man who used to live in the center of town, and this man was very quiet soul. He was missing an arm. He was an older man, maybe in his 70's or more, and he lived down a long winding path in the corner of town in a shack with no electricity, and no running water.

As children, we were fascinated about this man who only had one arm, and we would make up stories about what we thought his life was like and how he lost his arm. It may sound heartless, but for children who had never seen anyone with one arm, it was bound to happen, as nothing is more vivid than the imagination of a child. Another reason we were so interested in him may be because he didn't talk to us and because he didn't smile at you when you went by... so as children, we labeled him as someone who was pretty scary.

One of the things that we would do as kids, (as most kids did back then, and who knows, they probably still do now,) is that we challenged each other to be brave. One of those challenges was to go down that long path, down by the bog that wound through the woods to the shack. And the main challenge that seemed the scariest was to not get caught by the man with one arm. One day, it was my turn to go down the trail to see how far I could go, the goal being to get close enough to see the shack. Down the trail I went, slowly, cautiously, looking around each corner wondering if I was going to be approached by this man who had never spoken to me. To my own amazement, I made it all the way down and I could see the shack. My heart was racing, and I was so proud of my accomplishment. I was even prouder of the fact that I was able to do it and not get caught! So, I turned around and started working my way back up the path to where my friends were waiting at the top of the knoll. But lo and behold, I came around one of the corners and who was standing there but the man who lived in the shack! I stood there, barely breathing, not knowing what to say or what to do as this man looked at me. He was probably wondering why I was down here by his shack. My heart was racing as you can imagine because all those imaginary thoughts were going through my head wondering what he was going do to me, this man with the one arm who didn't speak to people. As I stood there, the man looked at me and said, "Did you make it to the shack?" "Yes sir," I said, "all the way down to it. It is your house, isn't it? I promise you I didn't do anything, I just looked at the shack." The man with one arm looked at me, and then he did something I had never seen him do before, he smiled at me. All of a sudden, my vision of this man softened and changed, it changed because he smiled down at me. And he said to me, "Maybe the next time you come down, you'll actually stop and say hello." I just stood there with my big brown eyes open wide and nodding my head up and down in disbelief... I was actually talking to this man. You see, of course this man knew the children were coming down spying on his house. I'm sure he heard all the giggles that took place as they turned around and ran back up the path to the road in the middle of town. I think back now to how sad this man may have been thinking that the children were all afraid of him because he was missing an arm. But my vision of this man changed that day all because of that one smile. Then the man stepped aside on the path, and waved his hand to say that I was able to pass by, and I ran as fast as I could up to where my friends were supposed to be waiting at the top of the trail. But when I arrived at the top of the trail, all my friends were gone. You see, they saw the man with one arm coming home and starting down the trail and knew that I was down there, and they ran away so they wouldn't get caught.

I moseyed my way back to my house to see if my friends were waiting for me there, but they were nowhere to be found. So, then I went over to another friend's house to see if I could catch up with them at their house. I wanted to share my story of meeting up with the man on the path, and that I made it all the way down to the shack. The funny thing was, when I found my friends, they all thought that I was making up a story. They believed there was no way that the man had approached me and smiled at me when he found me on the trail down to his shack. You see, I was known to have quite a vivid imagination as a little girl. I could make up some doozies of a story thinking how it would be so terrific if some of these imaginary stories came true.

I'm not surprised they just said, "Sure, Karen, another one of your stories." Ha, ha, ha.

So, there it was, my friends didn't believe me, but I knew that I had the chance to speak to the man with one arm on his path down to his shack that day. Later on in the week, my friends and I were down at the corner store. I was there to pick up something for my mom that she needed for supper. There was this same one-armed man sitting at the counter on a stool all by himself. Now the counter was located next to the cash register, so I was getting pretty close to where this man was sitting and my heart was racing, but I was going to show my friends that I actually did talk to the man with one arm. So, as I walked towards the counter, he saw me out of the corner of his eye. He slowly turned on the stool that he was sitting on, and the man smiled at me. "Good afternoon, young lady," he said. And I smiled back at the man, and I said, "Good afternoon, sir." Boy, my friends were really surprised to see me having a conversation with this man. They stood there with their mouths open wide staring at each other in disbelief. I proudly took my bag of groceries for my mom and stood up straight and tall as I walked past my friends knowing that I showed them. I proved that I did talk with the man with one arm, and that he did smile at me.

As time went on, when I would see this man come walking down past my house, I would go out on the lawn and wait for him to go by so that I could say hello. He had such a great smile, and there was something about him that just made you feel special when he would say hello back. I truly think this was the first encounter that I had of understanding not to label someone as being scary because they're different. To this day, I do not know this man's story of how he lost his arm, but I know how courageous he was and how much he changed my life. By taking that moment to see him as the person he was and stop labeling him as the person with one arm, I opened a door to where he became a friend. Because I started chatting with the man, some of the other children started to speak with him as well, and we would look for him when we went to the corner store just so we could say hello. It made me sad to think that other people, including myself prejudged him and were afraid of him because he was different. I think that encounter with me changed his life a lot too because the kids would stop and take the time to speak to him after that. They began to visit with him from time to time. It's amazing what one encounter can do to change the life of another, or even for oneself. By having my eyes opened to the person, and not to the image that I was seeing, and not understanding why he was different has stayed with me throughout my life. I cannot recall it, but I hope that as a child I apologized to him for being afraid of him. He was such a gentle, kind soul with a kind smile and a green hat tipped to one side on his snowy white hair. I can still see him in his green dickie work pants, sitting on the swivel stool at the counter in the little general store where I grew up.

This encounter and experience is one of my rocks, or stones, in my memory garden of life. I am now building my own garden of memories like Rose taught us to do. These stones create the shape and foundation within the fabric of our lives. Each stone has a unique shape and meaning that has carried me throughout life, a steppingstone that now has become an imprint to my soul and support for the trails to come.

By having a change in heart through this experience, it changed my course in life. It altered my path that stayed with me throughout my life. This memory stone shown from the botanical gardens is how I envision my path was changed. Now my path is beyond the boundary of "labeling," and I took a new path of understanding, all created by the simple gift of a smile.

The Botanical Gardens of Maine

CHAPTER 2

THE FABRIC OF OUR MEMORIES

*"Cherish your visions and dreams as they are
the children of your soul; the blueprints of your
ultimate achievements."*

These words come from a book called, *The Maxwell Daily Reader*. This is a 365-day book of insights. I truly believe that our fabric in life is created by all the experiences we've had throughout our lifetime. All of these experiences, visions, and dreams create the fabric of our soul. And they become a reflection, or a path that one may travel while navigating their personal *walk in Rose's Garden*. When shared, these memories will open doors to our most treasured moments in life revealing the depths of our imprints, our blueprints in life.

I recall an experience that I once had when I was a young teenager growing up in my small hometown in western Maine. There was a freedom that we had back then, and we would go and explore places in and around the town throughout the day. One place was a place called Devil's Den. Down the trail you would find this amazing gorge forged out of rocks and a waterfall that came from the gorge that went down to this beautiful pool of water. As kids, we would slide down these waterfalls and play in the pool at the bottom of the falls. But some of the most exciting times were around the challenges that we made with each other on the cliffs of the gorge.

Amongst the cascade, some of the smaller plunges at Devil's Den pass about 100 feet down through an attractive gorge to what people have expressed as looking like something out of Jurassic Park movie, as it was prehistoric and pristine. And in this gorge, there's an area that becomes a perfect cliff jumping spot that attracted us kids to see how far down we could go into the black waters of Devil's Den. It has been said that no one has ever touched the bottom at Devil's Den. And so it was, on warm summer days, we would ride our bikes towards South Arm and go to Devil's Den to jump from the cliffs and see how far down we could go.

Anyone who knows me knows how much I love the water, but the funny thing is, I'm not one to go under the water the way I used to as a child. I truly think that the story I'm about to share with you is the reason why I do not like to put my head under water.

One afternoon, all of us kids were lined up to run across the top of the cliff and jump out as far as we could to clear the rocks. We were cheering each other on, and then it became my turn to make the jump. I took a deep breath and off I went down over the side of the cliff. I hit the water, using my arms, I kept on pushing myself further and further down into the gorge. We would count the seconds so that we could compare our times to each other when we came back up to see how far we had gone down. As I was going down into the deep black water, I could hear everybody yelling ... one 1000, two 1000, three 1000, counting the seconds to mark how far down I was able to go. I knew I couldn't go any further, and I started to work my way up to the top of the water, but something scary started to happen. We had had some rain earlier that day, and the waters were running pretty fast at the bottom of that gorge.

Devil's Den

As I was looking up, I could see the small lit area at the top of the water that I was trying to reach, but as I was going up and up, my head kept on hitting the side of the gorge, as the water was pushing me underneath the side of the cliff. I started to realize I was losing my breath and I wasn't sure if I was going be able to make it to the top. Then, suddenly, I had a second breath that filled my lungs, and I floated up to the top of the water. To this day, I say that it felt like someone was blowing air into my lungs to help me to get to the top of the water. I'll never forget the feeling of lifelessness, like I just didn't have another ounce of strength to be able to carry through to reach the top of the water.

When I finally reached the top, I was completely exhausted, and I let the water carry me down over the little cascade of waterfalls that came out from the gorge.

So, you see, this became an imprint on the memories of my soul. Somewhere deep within my memory, every time that I am under water, I still reflect back to the time that I wasn't able to get to the top. Maybe this is why to this day I don't like to go under water because of that one experience at Devil's Den. This has become one of my memory stones, a part of my personal walk through Rose's Garden forming from within my own life, my memories. This type of memory stone of "fear" has been something I have seen people revisit while in their final transitions in life. This is a very deep type of stone that travels deep within the soul. Having the knowledge of these types of experiences is key in helping people open doors and calm the soul, especially during the final transitions in life. This next story will share the vivid reality of how "fear" can live deep within our soul.

I have witnessed some amazing experiences while working in our hospice programs over the years. If you've had the opportunity to read my book, *The Runner Who Never Ran: A Game Warden's Daughter*, you might recall the stories that I shared about the programs that we developed around a walk and Rose's Garden. This is another one of those stories that shows the importance of learning one's life story.

In one of our communities, we worked with individuals with memory impairment. We discovered the importance of learning one's life story to help our residents navigate life with this diagnosis and to help them be successful. We focused on their abilities, and their gem stones in life that were held so dear to them that they were imprinted on their soul. By being able to recite periods of their lives, and to know the names of those who they held dear, we saw that when they were transitioning through the end of life how astounding it was to have this knowledge to help them navigate their pathway.

We cared for a lovely lady who had an amazing life of courage and perseverance. She had grown up in Germany and was a young girl during WWII. Being Jewish, she and her sister needed to find a way to leave the country. So, she and her sister, with help from the underground, worked their way through secret passages and locations over the mountains to safety. The sad thing was that her sister did not survive the journey, and this was a huge imprint in this lady's soul. I cannot imagine the fear and courage it took to endure this undertaking, but during that time, it was an act of survival undertaken by many.

It came to the point in her life that she was transitioning through the end of life and her journey was reflecting upon times that none of us could imagine. But the thing we knew was her sister's name and that this lady had survived the journey and came to America. Her long-term memory was very intact and we would make sure, while caring for her, that everyone involved knew about her family, mother, and father, and that she had a sister that was very dear to her. It came to a point in her transitioning that she was clearly visiting the time in life when she was escaping from Germany. She was now speaking in German and her respirations were elevated. We could hear her asking about or searching for her sister. By using the care approach of her life story, a narrative medicine, we were able to comfort her by assuring her that her sister (by name) was okay, and that she was waiting for her. We would watch her respirations slow down and her anxiety soften all by knowing the fabric of her life's path. This fabric of her life story was a memory stone that ran deep within her soul. Her walk in Rose's Garden had a pathway of courage, fear, and perseverance beyond our imagination. This lady had a soul of memory stones that took her over mountains to safety. I will never forget the tears of the caregivers and their gentle voices assuring her that her sister was waiting for her and that they would be together again. Narrative medicine* soothed her soul and gave her a peaceful walk through her last moments in her passage of life.

Our imprint, or our life memories, are deeply rooted within our own personal walk in Rose's Garden. I feel it is important to know our family history and to share or record our journey so that our narrative journey is there to assist us in life. I have had well respected, professional businessmen in the healthcare field share with me that we were practicing a care approach well beyond our time. Narrative medicine was the key that opened the doors to a kinder parting and honored their journey.

TRANSFORM HEALTHCARE ONE STORY AT A TIME

Arising at Columbia University in 2001, narrative medicine has developed principles and practices that equip clinicians to better comprehend their patients' experiences and perspectives to deliver equitable and effective health care. Narrative medicine also engages with writers, artists, scholars, activists, and human services professionals of all kinds to improve health care from the perspectives of patients and providers.

Working with nurses, social workers, physicians, mental health professionals, chaplains, academics, and everyone interested in person-centered, respectful health care, this discipline aims to deepen self-awareness, clinical effectiveness, collaborative skills, and creative capacities through rigorous narrative training and practices.

Rarely do we imagine that one's rock memory garden is linear and precise... life just does not present life's lessons if everything is perfect and precise.

I believe our lives have unique memory stones that are sometimes laid upon the surface and at other times are buried deep within our soul. These emotional memories carry our life's lessons, our treasures, and our character that make us who we are. They can even sprout new life from situations that one would have thought to have been a barrier to prevent progress.

My father always taught me to look at my surroundings as we navigate life. As a game warden, he was always assessing the situation around him. He would use this information to anticipate his next steps in whether or not he needed to intervene in a situation or to let things be. He would know the trail he was to take to get where he was going and the barriers that he would face along the way.

Memory Stones can even "Sprout New Life."

This same teaching and philosophy are the basis of narrative medicine. It encompasses the act of looking at one's abilities and factor in the memories of what has happened in the past as a way to navigate the trails ahead. This is what we saw time and time again in the communities that I managed as we helped people navigate their personal journey in Rose's Garden. The road of the reflection, and of our memories, have intertwined within our lives. Never underestimate the power of a memory in your life and how it relates to a certain result. This next story will amaze you as to how this shows up!

CHAPTER 3

THE MAGIC OF THE IMPRINTS IN OUR HEARTS

"One of the most important things about wisdom is that you can never have enough."
—by Paul L. Getter

These words are from a book a dear friend gave me, *Solomon's Success Code*, by Paul L. Getter. In his book, he describes the importance of wisdom and how by asking for it, it helps us navigate our path. It goes on to say...

"You face new challenges each day, so you need a new level of wisdom and understanding to face those challenges. Sure, you can refer to your past experiences, and that can be helpful to a point; but to be truly wise, you need to watch "daily at [wisdom's] gates [and wait' beside [her] doors. (Proverbs 8:34)"

He goes on to share that if we diligently seek wisdom, we may be more prepared than we thought we might be by this act of intentionally seeking wisdom each day. This story emphasizes those words...

A number of years ago, we admitted this lovely lady who had a stroke, which had left her with aphasia, and the inability to ambulate safely. But one of the most frustrating barriers she encountered was that she could not pronounce her words at all. This created very frustrating times for her where she could not communicate with anyone, and it would be so discouraging to her.

When she arrived, we had things set up for her as a replica of her bedroom at her own home, including some of her own furniture and paintings. This was a normal process for us as we had found that it created a calmer and kinder road to recovery. Once people were through their rehab with occupational therapy and physical therapy, their belongings would go back to their home with them so that they could continue their success in recovery.

We were making progress with her ambulatory capabilities, and speech therapy was assisting her to swallow and have better nutrition as she graduated from a soft diet to a solid one. But her aphasia was still discouraging to her as she could not communicate in a way that people could understand her. She would be in tears as she attempted to speak to us and to her devoted daughter trying to relay what she wanted. It broke our hearts to see how sad she was.

One day, the regular PT (Physical Therapist) was not available, and another PT stood in for her. This was perfectly fine as we knew her, and she was someone who worked in our community regularly. She was also someone who I knew personally, and I knew this resident would be in great hands and that she would love her temporary therapist.

The day came that PT was scheduled with her new therapist. On this particular day, the resident's daughter had tried to comfort her mother as it was one of those days that the resident was very depressed about her inability to communicate. We asked for the daughter to come in to be there to meet the new therapist and to provide comfort to her mother while meeting someone new.

I happened to be in the room to introduce the new therapist to the daughter and resident, along with our Director of Nursing. When we walked into the room the resident was in tears. She was so frustrated in trying to explain to her daughter what she wanted to wear, that the two of them were in tears.

Suddenly, the new physical therapist stopped in her tracks. She went over to the resident, knelt down on her knees beside her and reached for her hands to calm her. And then something amazing happened. The therapist started to speak in a different language to the resident. We all just stood staring at each other wondering what was going on. But then, the look on the face of the resident was one that I will never forget.

The tears that were flowing were now accompanied by a smile... she finally had someone who could understand what she was saying. Her aphasia was not an inability to communicate in the way that we all thought from the stroke. We thought she lost her ability to put letters together to form words. No, she was speaking in her childhood language from when she was a little girl. She was speaking in Dutch! None of us spoke this language so we had no idea that was the issue until the therapist made it clear to us.

Oh my goodness, you can imagine the excitement in the room as the therapist responded to her when she asked for this and for that. It was magical to say the least. Those weary, tear-filled eyes were now twinkling with joy that she wasn't left with an inability to communicate. She was just speaking in a different language from when she was a child!!

You see, that magical imprint from when she was a child, of her birthright language, was still there at her core. When she had her stroke, it created a barrier to the English language as an inability to speak English, but she could understand it, and she knew what she wanted to say in English. But when she tried vocalizing it, it came out in Dutch.

This change in the schedule to a new therapist was not an act of chance. I believe it was an answer to prayers, many prayers. This relationship with her new physical therapist transformed this lady's hope in life, along with her daughters. We taught specific words to the staff in Dutch to assist in caring for her. Over time, her English language capabilities returned to her. Her ambulatory gait improved, and she had many days filled with smiles and memories made with her friends and family. Miracles happen every day, and they bring us gifts to create memories one would have never thought possible.

This "hope" in life is a gift from my mother, as her wisdom in life was immeasurable.

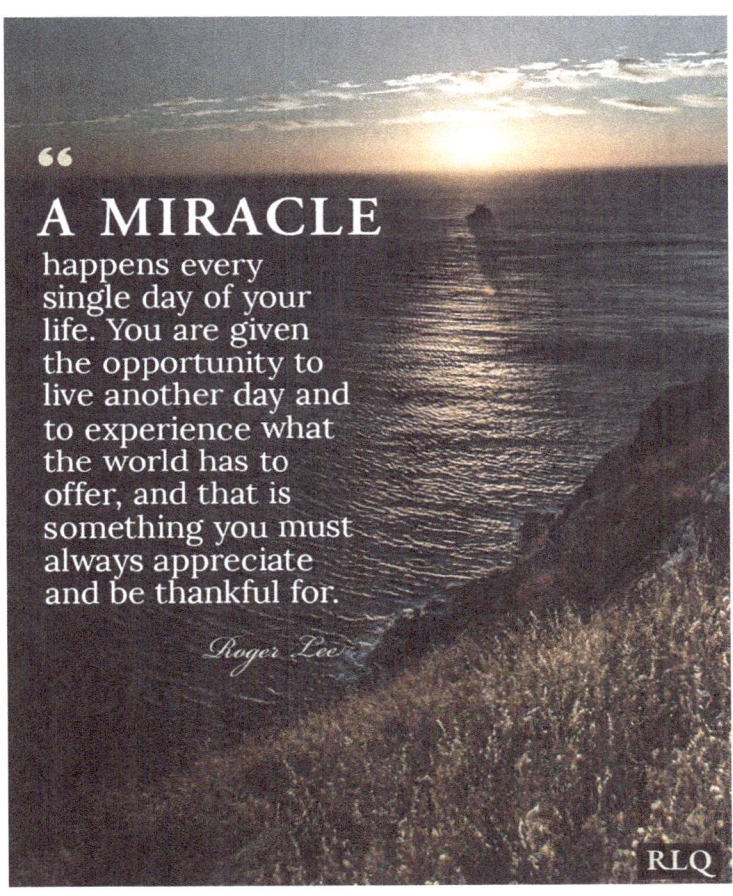

A MIRACLE happens every single day of your life. You are given the opportunity to live another day and to experience what the world has to offer, and that is something you must always appreciate and be thankful for.

Roger Lee

RLQ

CHAPTER 4

PATHS TRAVELED WILL LEAD TO DEEP MEMORIES

"They turned their stumbling blocks into stepping-stones. They realized they could not determine every circumstance in life, but they could determine their choice of attitude toward every circumstance."

These words were shared by John C. Maxwell in *Developing the Leader Within You.* This was a reflection of some famous leaders in our history. Helen Keller, Franklin Delano Roosevelt, Winston Churchill, Mahatma Gandhi, Albert Schweitzer, and Albert Einstein all revealed that one-fourth had handicaps, blindness, deafness or crippled limbs and three fourths had been born in poverty or broken homes and unsettling situations. They all learned to view their "problems" as temporary stumbling blocks, and they created paths traveled, which paved deep memories that many of us still reflect upon today.

As we reflect upon our own lives and our paths traveled, our Walk in Rose's Garden, our steppingstones in life reflect our own life story. These deep memories stay with us and as we transition through the end of life, this can be ever so present as you have read within these stories. This next story has its own place in history.

There was a gentleman who needed a place to go from the hospital, and people were hesitant to admit him due to his "behaviors" from his PTSD. His life had included highly stressful experiences that people did not take into consideration as the reason to his inability to cope with this world.

After speaking with his Power of Attorney and physicians, and meeting with our team to assess whether or not we were equipped to help him "transition" through his last stages of life, we started to focus on his life story. His diagnosis was that he had cancer, and he needed a place to have hospice services. We had learned that by understanding one's life history we could help those transitioning through their end stages of life, or as we referred to it, their path in Rose's Garden, so we started gathering information of his life history. We were determined that we would try to help this man and admitted him into our hospice program as he needed a place to go.

You see, this man was someone who fought in WWII during the time after Pearl Harbor and the war with the Japanese. He had the covert task of sneaking onto an island in the dark of night, scoping out the enemy and their forces. They would drop him off by submarine, and he would hide on the island gathering information for the battle that was being planned as an invasion to the island.

As you can imagine, this is an unimaginable task. To risk life and limb to hide amongst the enemy and to escape with your life to report to the commanders what the circumstances were and where the enemy strength lied prior to an attack by the US forces was a high-risk task. The island was Iwo Jima. This amphibious invasion was a costly victory for the United States, and the battle is known as one the bloodiest in the history of the U.S. Marine Corps. It is said that the battle was proof that the Japanese military would fight to the last man standing.

This man was part of a counteroffensive that incorporated a strategic combination of land, air, and naval assaults. This volcanic island covered about eight square miles with hundreds of caves all covered with volcanic sand and ash. The Japanese commanders constructed a network of tunnels beneath the island for protection and to circumvent enemy lines. The Japanese soldiers were in these tunnels and caves with an estimated 21,000 soldiers.

The reason I share all this is that we had to learn this story to care for our newly admitted resident as caregivers. This man would have nightmares and become hypersensitive to noise was living in a world that was a repeated chapter of his time on that island. He was reliving it daily. By knowing the steppingstones of his life, we were able to monitor dates, activities, and storms that may trigger his memory path of deep emotions. His unsettling experiences were occurring in his mind as he was transitioning through his final stages in life. By us knowing his tapestry in life and his heroism was an important key to his journey. This dear man saved so many lives during this operation. We wanted to honor his life as best we could by helping him through this stage in life with the information we had, so we could provide some comfort to his journey.

My own father served in the Pacific theater, and I remember when he would have returned bouts of malaria. That disease never left him and while in the throes of the illness, he would revisit those memories on those islands. I recall my mother saying, "He's okay, he is reliving memories that were horrific, and he will be okay once the fever breaks." I remember my mother reassuring him, calming his memories and fears. This same technique was used with our gentleman as well by reassuring him that he was successful and that he made it out to warn the troops. The staff would sit with him, as my mother would with my father, and calm his soul through these deep memories as he transitioned through his pathway of life. It is said that one of the most concerning things about that battle was the fact that the JCOS (Joint Chiefs of Staff) did not consider the "opinions" of the Marines or the doubts of their planners ahead of ordering the invasion. Had they done so, it is said that thousands of lives might have been saved. We often wondered if this was one of the biggest struggles of this man's walk through his pathway in hospice. Was he one of those Marines who carried that information to those he needed to report to only to find that they did not heed his word? I cannot imagine his journey nor his visions that must have taunted him.

By knowing the life story and honoring this man's life, he was able to receive a measure of peace at end of life.

Never underestimate the power of human kindness and the ever "knowing" that one can give through the trials of life. This information and acknowledgment allowed this gentleman to pass with dignity and with the respect that he so deserved.

Again, like the stories I shared in my book *The Runner Who Never Ran: A Game Warden's Daughter* this same angel teaching that my mother passed to me as a child was once more ever present. Each story was a steppingstone through all the doors that the angels had prepared for us to know. My prayer was that he visited a kinder vision of the beautiful Japanese island and walked a more tranquil journey through his pathway in life on steppingstones that reflect peace and happiness and to find tranquility around the bend.

Japanese Garden Path

I have had more times than I can count people sharing with me, "If I had only known that by playing that favorite song, or by whispering the story of their favorite trip that one had taken, that this would have softened their journey, I would have done it."

My goal was, and is, to equip our loved ones with the tools to soften our journey in life. Honor the life once traveled and embrace the gift of opening doors that once was closed... embrace the journey and reveal your path taken.

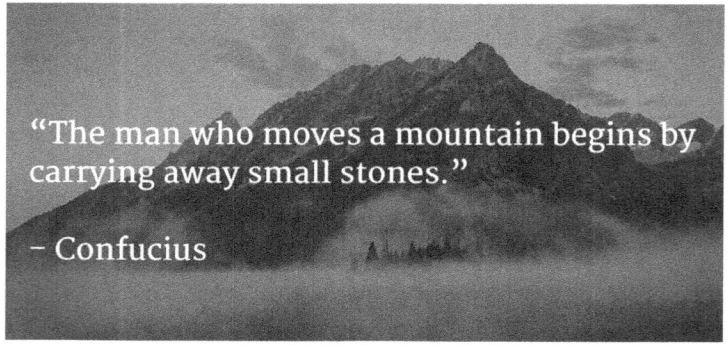

To achieve something substantial, we must begin by taking small steps towards it. Many of us make a mistake of thinking that if we take a few giant leaps, we will reach our goal faster.
—Confucius

Confucius had principles that fostered a strong family loyalty, a respect of elders by their children with the concept that family is a basis for ideal government. Home is a person's castle, a place of refuge. He stood by the principle of "Do not do unto others what you do not want done to yourself." The Golden Rule of life.

These principles are ever present as a focus of intentionally looking to the needs of others as way of honoring their life as we did with this gentleman you just met. Each memory stone that we acknowledge, no matter how small, is an imprint to our lives. Honor your journey and embrace the gift that it is and remember to share your story.

CHAPTER 5

THE TREASURES FROM OUR HERITAGE

"He will cover you with His feathers, and under His wings you will find refuge."
—Psalm 91:4

This next story is one that my father shared with me when I was a little girl. It was first told to him by his mother, my Nana. There was once a beautiful old New England style home in Standish, Maine that belonged to my father's grandmother's family, my great-great-grandmother, Mary France Bradbury, born in 1850, known as the Bradbury homestead. It was a home with family antiques and many memories of yesteryear full of family heirlooms and treasures.

This home neighbored my Nana's home. My Nana's home was a working home that took in boarders and traders who came into town in the early 1900's. My Nana had two men that worked for her, one was the gardener and handyman who was a short and stout man, and the other was a very tall man who people would say was a walking refrigerator and as strong as an ox. These two men would work the apple orchards and harvest the gardens as my Nana took care of the home and cooked meals for the boarders who came to stay at her boarding home.

The Swasey Home on Oak Hill Road.

You see, my Nana lived alone and raised my Dad and his sister Mary by herself as she lost my grandfather when my Dad was only 12 years old. My grandfather was an attorney by profession, as was his father and grandfather. They had an office at the Bradbury home where they kept the town's ledger of all the births, land deeds, and marriages and court proceedings.

As you look at the picture of the Swasey home, you can imagine how the Bradbury home might have looked; it was located in the open area that you can see in this picture. As the story is told, it was a New England farmhouse with an attached barn similar to my Nana's home.

In the early years of the 1900's, the town of Standish had a dev-astating event with houses being set on fire. There were three homes, all in this same vicinity that were set on fire by an ar-sonist. I can just imagine the fear that the townspeople must have had wondering if their home was to be next to be set on fire. Then it happened, the next fire was the Bradbury house, my great-great-grandmother's homestead. I cannot imagine the heat, heartache, and fear that my Nana, my father, and my Aunt Mary must have had seeing this take place. My father was a young boy at this time and didn't recall much of that night accept of a miracle that occurred that night that he could never forget.

The townspeople all came to fight the fire, and they were also trying to save my Nana's farm as well as it was so close by. But then, on this day, something amazing happened that no one could believe.

You remember I shared with you that the home contained an-tiques and family heirlooms along with town documents. The office that my grandfather and his father had used as an attorney along with so many family heirlooms were burning. Dad told me he could remember Nana being so upset that all those precious memories and heirlooms would be lost forever in the fire.

Then, something incredible happened. Remember the short, stout man that was the handy man for my Nana? Well, he ran into the burning building and when he came out, he was carry-ing a large lawyer's bookcase that had so many of the old docu-ments and treasured books. "Picture a man," Dad would tell me," five foot nothing, carrying a large lawyer's oak bookcase full of books out of a burning building and placing it on the lawn out front of the home." It is an absolute miracle that he could lift that heavy bookcase. I did some research about the approximate weight of lawyer bookcases of that era, and this is what I found.

They say an average weight of a lawyer's bookcase such as this weighs approximately 700 lbs. Imagine being able to pick it up and carry it out of a burning building. Angels at work I say because if it wasn't for the gift of strength to carry that bookcase out of the building, I would not have the following items today.

Because of this event and unbelievable courage and heart to protect the heirlooms of my family, I have the gift of holding my grandfather, Joseph T. Swasey's, Bible from 1896 given to him by his mother, my great-great-grandmother.

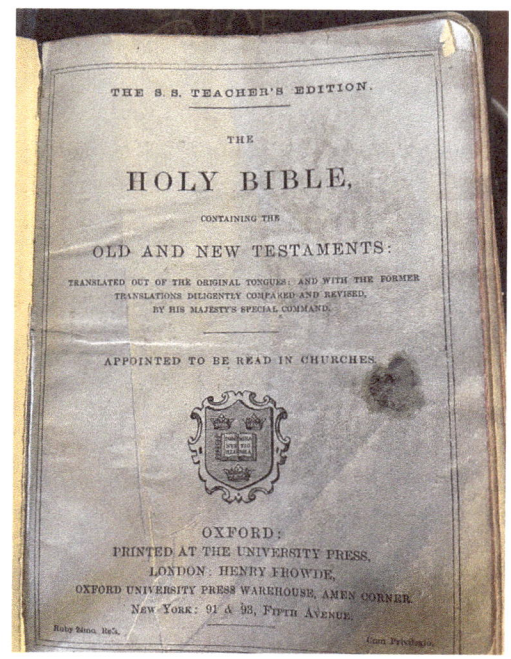

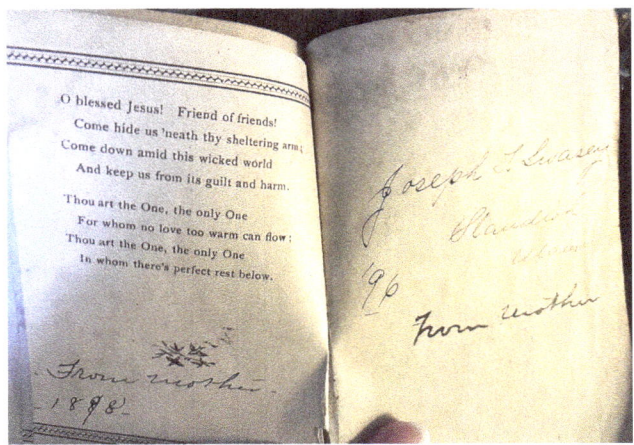

Inside is a poem given to him that is signed, Mother.

This Bible is 127 years old, and the pages are crisp and thin but so preserved with love. If it wasn't for that kind man running into that burning building, I would have never been able to hold this treasure in my own hands. To hold it is a feeling beyond words. It is like holding a fragile bird in my hands, I treasure it so. But that wasn't all that was in the bookcase; I have the book that belonged to my great grandfather from the early 1800's that has an elegant gold binding and thick leather-embossed cover. I have his Charles Dicken's collections and poetry books by Tennyson dated from 1899. I also have the ledger that has the case registry of legal hearings dated back to 1876, all in the pen of my great-great-great-grandfather. In it is this entry that marks the day that my great-great-great-grandfather passed.

> *"These works number 190 and number 191*
> *were drawn by my dear father on Wednesday,*
> *August 23, 1882, with all care possible and in a*
> *hand as fair firm, and legible as ever penned by*
> *him. The officer (name) that he received the writ*
> *that day from father with careful and precise*

directions as to the attachment of personal estate made by him. Cautious, careful and precise in the morning of his business career, dear father in his mature experience exercised always without varying the utmost accuracy and the most prudent means."
"Rest Well," Written by Charles F. Swasey

Oh, how the tears flowed reading this entry that has been preserved so that I have had this connection to this moment in time. You see, that solitary act of saving those treasures and records has given the gift of having the writings in my own great-great-great-grandfather's pen is something that cannot be duplicated. I believe that these gifts are a confirmation of how the tapestry of my life is formed. The honor, the respect, and the courage to persevere is deeply rooted within my soul. I believe that these items were meant to be known by my children's, children as a thread of history in their own lineage's pen. Within these pages, I am able read the stories of life's memories from so long ago. And now I get to keep them within my own steppingstones of life, my Walk in Rose's Garden, as my family's history is so preserved as to live on through years to come.

"But the story continues....."

The amazing thing is, a similar thing happened on my mother's side of the family. My mother lost her mother when she was 12 years old, so all I have in knowing her are the stories my mother would share with me. She would share about how much faith she had, and she had the voice of a songbird. This must be where my mother received her gift of having a beautiful voice, along with the gift of playing the piano. My mother would share the stories of faith that her mother had shared with her as a child and how her mother taught her to play the piano. Oh, how I treasure those memories that my mother would share and listening to my mother play the piano.

As years went by, my mother's brother, Uncle Bob, was raising his family in the Heggeman homestead that coincidentally, was just across the road from where my father grew up. You see, my mother lived on what is now route 25 now in Standish, Maine in the center of town, and my father grew up on Oak Hill Road right across the way in plain view of each other. It is funny to think how they could look at each other's houses when they were children, and it makes one wonder if they ever spent time together as children. Mom nor Dad never really spoke about it, except the stories of when Mom worked the telephone office in a small building in the middle of town, and Dad was known to visit her. Everyone I have ever met who knew of my mother as a young lady commented on how beautiful she was, and they would always remark about her beautiful red auburn hair. And so it was, childhood friends were married on August 3, 1946.

In this same house where my mother grew up, my Uncle Bob, my mom's brother, lived and raised his family. My Uncle Bob had a deep passion and skill of working with antique cars. He had the most amazing antique car collection that he kept in the big barn attached to the old homestead. In there, he had model Ts and other antique cars that he worked on and would go for a drive in with the love of his life, my Aunt Priscilla. One sad night, the barn caught fire and they lost a number of the cars, but that is not the only thing that was stored in this barn, it also held the box of heirlooms of my mother's mother.

In the aftermath of the fire, everyone thought all was lost of these heirlooms, and they were not to be held again. But the Good Lord had something else in mind, and those angels were at work again, as my mother would say. I remember the day that my Aunt Priscilla came to the house to bring something to my mother. She came into the house with this box and placed it on the kitchen table. Could it be? This box was perfectly preserved, it was not scorched or damaged in any way. I remember the disbelief in my mother's eyes as she touched the box. I then realized whose box this was as the tears were coming down my mother's face. As she opened the box, there inside were my Nana Heggeman's recipe books, letters, and one very special item, her Bible. They were all preserved without a mark. Now mind you, these items were all stored in the barn that burned.

When they went through the soot and wreckage from the fire, they were searching for the box that held these heirlooms, and they said they lifted up something and there, underneath the debris, was this box. Not scorched or damaged by the water but preserved as if protected by the love that was inside.

Tears flowed in amazement as to how these items were protected from the fire and water. I will never forget this day as my mother showed me these treasures; pure joy radiated over my mother's face while holding these memories from so long ago. And now the gift I have is that I can place my hands on these items today. Holding the Bible that my mother was given in 1937 by her mother is a treasure that one cannot express. Seeing the inscription in my Nana Heggeman's pen to my mother is priceless. Knowing that this was protected from the fire and water so that my mother could hold those items from so long ago, and now, I have this same opportunity to share with my own children.

My mother always told me that angels are all around if we would only take the time to be present and listen and hear from our heart. This gift to my mother is something that I believe the angels delivered to her so that she could hold those items that meant so much to her mother.

I remember being told that my grandmother had a faith that never faltered. All through her time of being sick with cancer at a young age in her 40s, her faith was her strength. My mother would share with me stories of strength that her mother had enduring her journey with cancer. She told me that she would sit with her, and her mother would tell her not to worry as Jesus was with her and the angels are all around. I believe this is where I get my sense of angels, from my dear Nana Heggeman, who passed this gift to my mom so many years ago.

Florence Muriel Miller Heggeman was born in 1900 and passed in 1944 in her home in Standish, Maine. She was born in Camp-belton, New Brunswick in Restigouche County, Canada. And the reason I know this, is that when I had identical twin girls that were identified as identical mirror twins, we found out that the only way identical mirror twins can occur, is when it is passed down through the maternal genes. My mother was so excited to find this out that she researched her family history with her siblings to see what they could find. Come to find out, identical twin girls were born with beautiful red hair, and they were mirror twins. They were born in Canada in New Brunswick on my mother's, mother's side of the family. Now I would say... her presence is still strong today! My mother was so tickled to know that her granddaughters with beautiful red auburn hair was passed down from her dear mother so many years ago.

So, these are the stories of my heritage, of angels who gave protection over my family's heirlooms of memories, dear treasures each and every one. Two separate incidents of heirlooms being protected from fire that are perfectly preserved for my children's children to treasure is heaven sent. Items to be treasured and honored as the gifts that they are... memory stones sharing their pathways of life.

Yes, one may say that these are "only things," material items, but to me, they once had the hands of my grandparents touching them and writing messages of a life lived are scribed inside. To me, this is a blessing one cannot describe. These are the stepping-stones of my heritage divinely delivered so that I may hold them in my own hands and learn from them, the gifts of old. These pages reflect the fabric of my soul, my faith, my ingenuity, my courage, and my inspiration given to me by the angels of my ancestors. Oh, how grateful I am to reflect upon these memory paths set before me, a reflection of a life once lived, a true treasure of the heart.

Embrace your journey. You never know what
gifts are waiting for you around the corner

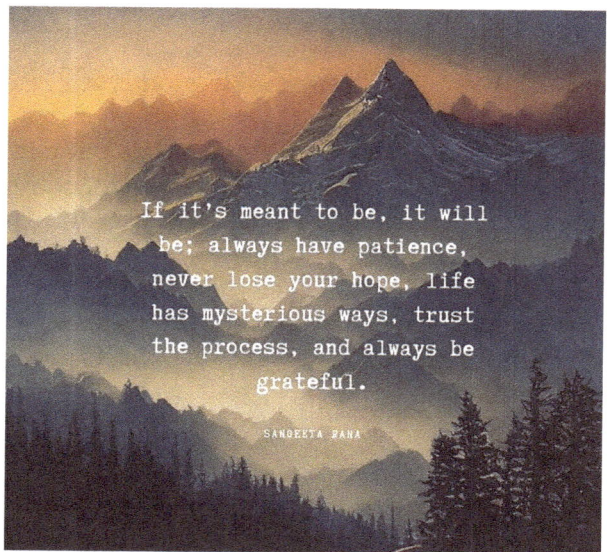

If it's meant to be, it will be; always have patience, never lose your hope, life has mysterious ways, trust the process, and always be grateful.

SANDEETA RANA

CHAPTER 6

STEPPINGSTONES OF PURPOSE

"A bend in the road is not the end of the road...
unless you fail to make the turn."
—*Author Unknown*

People I know are forever telling me that they are amazed to the number of "God Winks" that I have in my life. I believe it is the gift from my Mom who always asked me to be on the lookout for angels in my life. I can remember one time when I was getting into my car and as I closed the door, I was suddenly startled by a cardinal that landed on my car's side mirror. There it was, just looking in at me through the window. Boy, did I have goose bumps all over me! I knew at that moment that I was experiencing a gift delivered from my mom. She had always told me that a visit from a cardinal was a visit from an angel. To this day, I have cardinals all around me. I hear them on my walks, while I am sitting in my yard, and it is amazing seeing how many times they pass in front of me when I am driving. I think they are reminding me that they are always with me no matter where I go.

There is one occasion of a visit from a cardinal I will never forget. It was when my mother passed a number of years ago. We had a cardinal come to the window of her room the moment she passed. My brother said to us, "Look over here," as he was standing at the window. There was a cardinal sitting on the windowsill. It came right up to the window, as all five of us stood there in the window looking at it in amazement. It then turned and looked up, and then it flew up to a branch.

As we followed it up into the tree, there was another cardinal waiting for it up high in the tree. It was just as though she was joining Dad, and then the two of them flew off up into the sky. It still takes my breath away every time I think of it. She sent this gift to us to show us that she had been set free, and she showed us that she was with Dad now. These cardinals had a purpose for each one of us in the room knowing that she had now embraced her joy and was no longer hurting or feeling sad, engulfed me. She was set free; and as I reflect back upon the visit from the cardinal, it was so fitting as her angel. Mom always had such a deep love for cardinals, and she would light up every time she saw one.

She had a deep love and appreciation for two specific birds that I remember in her life, one was her cardinals (which were angels to her sent as messengers from above) and the second bird was her loons. Oh, how she loved her loons at camp.

Northern Loon

Mom would sit on the point at camp and call to her loons in the evening as the sun went down. It would always amaze me to see how the loons would come into the cove to visit her as she called out to them. Thinking of it this now, it prompted me to look up the meaning of her loons and what they may have been bringing into her life.

Her loons are known as symbolizing tranquility, serenity, and the reawakening of old hopes, wishes and dreams. This resembled mom's nature to a T, as she always shared with me the message that I am to always follow my hopes, wishes, and dreams. Maybe these visits with her loons enlightened her to share this with me, as they must have brought peace and tranquility to her.

Camp was always her refuge and her place of tranquility, and just maybe, the visits from the loons helped that become a reality to her.

So now with each visit that I have from a cardinal, I smile, and pause to notice the gift. And in the night, as I lay in bed, I hear the loons on the lake singing their songs to each other in the light of the moon.

I reminisce of mom and of all the stories that she shared with me as each story holds a very dear place in my heart.

A Message from Heaven, a visit from a Cardinal

A gentle reminder that we're never far apart.
My spirit will live on forever
there within your heart.

And when you see a cardinal,
here to brighten your day,
remember that I'm there with you,
and there I'll always stay.

I truly believe we are to always acknowledge these moments in our lives, these "God Winks" that are being sent from above. And no matter what belief you may hold as part of your journey, these gifts are there for you to hold.

They are the tapestry of our beings that carry memories of old. And when I travel through my final stages of life, I believe, and I have seen it to be true, that these memories become ever so vibrant again. All these special memories are the keys within my soul, and they complete my visions, hopes, and dreams. These gifts of old in being able to hold and read messages from my deep heritage of years past are a treasure to bestow. They hold memories of my forefathers that now I have the duty to pass onto my own children, so that they may have a glimpse of their heritage and who they were, their hopes, wishes, and dreams.

I have seen that within the final days of our lives we visit these memory stones of life, each person's personal journey as you Walk in Rose's Garden. Their path may be that of a solider who was an unknown hero delivering vital information to save troops, or of two sisters who escaped from horrific circumstances by traveling and hiding across mountains to try to get to a place of hope and a new beginning. Or it may be how someone had an experience of a medical event and lost their ability to communicate, or so they thought, as she was speaking in her birthright language of Dutch. These all become imprints of our memories, and they become the memory stones of our lives.

It is so very important to recognize these memories and honor them as the imprints of one's soul. When one starts to travel through their Walk in Rose's Garden, it is essential for them to have the support and the knowing that their life story is being remembered. The gift of knowing one's life story becomes the key to the journey that one will take in their final transition in this life. Each garden is unique to each person's life experiences as you have read in these pages. Having someone with the knowledge of these keys or steppingstones of memories is essential in opening the doors of a peaceful transition. I believe the gift of having someone present, who understands who you truly were in life, who knows your life story, and honors that memory, will help one navigate their journey through Rose's Garden.

We all have our journey to tell. The dreams, wishes, and hopes that we have experienced in life. Your journey through the memory stones of Rose's Garden is yours alone. Each stone carries the depths of our memories. Some lay on the surface and are a whisper of a memory, and other stones are deep down within our soul. Those stones become our imprints of memories, and they hold the keys to our life story.

"Keys of Life"

I found this to be so true when a dear friend (now professor) and I presented a training to my staff in a memory care facility I managed.

The training was called, "The Keys of Life." We had the staff come into the room and once everyone was seated, my training partner said, "Now, Karen is going to come around with a basket and I want you to put all your belongings in the basket that are in your pockets." As I went around the room, each staff member would hesitate as they took their belongings out of their pockets, and I would say, "Oh, it's okay, I will take good care of these things for you." I would smile and entice them to put the items into the basket. They really didn't want to let go of these things. You see, these items were keys to their homes, or keys to their car to get home, or a cell phone in case their child may call if they needed something. They were their "keys" to their access of life, their home, and all things treasured. Once I had the belongings in the basket, I went to the front of the room. I smiled at them, and then left the room.

My training partner remained there looking at the staff who were very unsettled. They knew me, and they trusted me, but their "keys" to their lives were out of sight. One staff member spoke up, "I really need her to come back in here, what if my daughter calls and needs something?" Another said, "Okay, she can bring them back in now." They all were very unsettled. My training partner said, "What's wrong? Don't you trust her?" And they said, "yes, but I need to have them back, so I know that they didn't get taken anywhere. I can't get home to my child or get into the house without my keys."

My training partner just sat there letting them feel the emotions they were having… and then, I came through the door without the basket. The body language in the room was evident in that emotions were running high. And then we asked, "How do you feel right now?" They said, "Scared, angry, lost, and uneasy," and one said, "I want to know what you did with my things!"

I looked at my training partner then I left the room and brought the basket back into the room. We sat in front of the staff and asked a very important question. "How do you think each resident with memory loss feels when we bring them into our facility? Do you think they probably feel the same way you are feeling right now?" They all started to look at each other. "The residents have lost the physical 'keys' to their lives, and they are not able to go home to get them. No one is bringing them in a basket so they can leave and go home to their families."

The staff just sat there dumbfounded, some with tears welling up, now understanding in that moment what this training was all about. We then discussed how the resident that they admitted that day might have felt as the staff were saying to her, "It will be alright, don't worry, I have everything taken care of for you. You're okay!"

From that moment on, there was a difference in how the staff embraced the "keys" of knowing the resident's life story upon an admission. They now knew and embraced how important the "keys" to who the residents were as a person was as they felt it themselves after taking this training. Those words in their life story were the keys to who they were as a person, their profession, their family, where they were born, their favorite hobby, and where they raised their family. Names of sisters, brothers, parents, children, and pets were all used as comforting tools of having someone "know" who they were as a person and not defined in life by their "diagnosis." They learned all the imprints of their memories that each resident holds and honored it as their personal walk in Rose's Garden. I had staff express how it changed their own lives after attending that training and how they had a better understanding of the gift of having "The Keys of Life" within their grasp.

This model was embraced from that day forward to the importance it held. It reduced episodes of anxiety, it gave joy, and it helped those transitioning through their final stages of life. This was a kinder practice of hospice, of caring for those with memory loss and of honoring one's life.

I believe we should all have a place where we have our memory stones, the imprints of our soul written down so one would know who we were and what hopes, wishes and dreams we had.

Writing your Walk in Rose's Garden is a gift to those you love. We have saved some pages at the end of this book for you to write your "Memory Stones" of life. The imprint that gives you purpose and identifies your memories. Find a picture of your Walk in Rose's Garden, your pathway, a reflection to leave as an image keepsake. Below is mine...

Memory Stones of a Path in Andover

I found this place one day with my husband enjoying a lovely fall day while renting a cabin along this beautiful brook. My path in Rose's Garden will look something like this, with crystal clear waters with the gentle sound of rippling water as it flows over the rocks in the stream. Here will be my memories of my beautiful girls being born and the stories of my heritage being shared with my grandchildren. The memories of my childhood growing up in a small town with friends and family all around. One could read such stories in my book, *The Runner Who Never Ran: A Game Wardens Daughter* and have pieces of my life story. The daughter who was thought to have left her hometown, but in her heart, she had never left, it was an imprint within her life, her hopes, wishes and dreams; it was the treasures of her soul.

So, now you have a glimpse of my "Keys of Life" and what may be written in my life story. They are now a part of my *"Walk in Rose's Garden,"* entwined within the memory stones of my life, an imprint of my memories.

Is it time to share yours; turn the page, it is time to explore.

CHAPTER 7

IMPRINTS IN OUR HEARTS

"Wisdom is the reward you get for a lifetime of listening when you would have preferred to talk."
—*Doug Larson*

It's said that listening is a learned skill. To have a teachable spirit is a learned practice as well. We grow in life by embracing these two habits as a daily practice, and they become our pillars of learning. Listening and applying each lesson until they become an imprint in our life by learning something new each day, your reward will be the gift of wisdom.

John Maxwell shares the writings of Marian Wright Edelman in his book, *Sometimes We Win, Sometimes We Learn*. He shares these thoughts that Marian wrote, "We must not, in trying to think about how we can make a big difference, ignore the small daily differences we can make which, over time, add up to big differences that we often cannot foresee." Oh, how true this statement is. It all arises by having a teachable spirit. Taking these daily experiences as treasures and applying each moment as an opportunity to walk through an open door of change. It may not reveal the message within the day, but as John shares, it will change your days for life.

This is what the imprints of our memories are all about. Experiences, opportunities, and embracing life's lessons along your journey, they all are the pillars of learning we embrace through life.

I think back to all the stories of people's lives that I have had the opportunity to learn from, and I take a deep breath of gratitude. Each story gave a glimpse into the lives of those we were blessed to take care of during my healthcare career. Meeting them would always prompt me to look up the "geography" of where their lives took place, to the time periods of what their lives would have been like, and challenges that they may have endured during that place in time.

I find it interesting that this trait or habit of having an interest in learning more of the geography is something that is a learned practice instilled in me since I was a child. The definition of geography is:

> *Geography is a field of science devoted to the study of lands, features, inhabitants, and phenomena of the earth. It derives from a Greek scholar Eratosthenes where it is explained as an encompassing discipline that seeks and understanding of the earth and natural complexities-not merely where objects are, but also how they have changed to come to be.*

The word "geography" is the core of one's life story, the tapestry of our lives in a word. It wasn't until now that I truly understood the correlation of the practice we used in our communities as the geography of one's life. It is the narrative medicine of understanding and acknowledging the wisdom that one has learned through their lives. Each turn in the road that those residents experienced became an imprint on their heart, the geography of their soul.

I look back into the memories of my own life to when I have experienced moments of losing my breath from the beauty I had seen before me. These are moments to what I believe is that expression of pure joy. I remember the time I was traveling out west with my mother, and we timed the arrival to watch the sunset at the Grand Canyon at a specific time. We traveled to Sun City to visit my Aunt Mary, my father's sister who now lived in Arizona. She had shared with us that we needed to be at a place called Mohave Point to experience a sunset that would take your breath away, and that it did!

Having that imprint of a memory with my mother is a treasure I will never forget. The gentle breeze that whispered through our hair as the majestic eagles soared in the sky from the updrafts of the air from the canyon below. It was breathtaking. And then there were the colors, all the arrays of a rainbow were there before us as the sun set on the rim. This gift is an imprint in my soul, and I can still see it clearly today.

This opportunity for my mother and I to visit Arizona was an invitation from my Aunt Mary. Mary A. Swasey Stewart was born in 1910 in Standish, Maine. She was my father's older and only sister. My Aunt Mary was a world traveler and a strong-minded soul. She and Uncle Walt traveled to all the corners of the earth exploring places with golf courses and majestic mountains and country sides of exploration. They especially loved Europe and the green lands of Ireland and Scotland. They would bring their traveling photos as slides each Christmas where we would share an evening of laughter and moments of amazement of where they had traveled. In my childhood, we used to switch off going to Aunt Mary's house in East Longmeadow, Massachusetts every other Christmas. This small-town girl having the excitement of going to the big cities, like Hartford, Connecticut, was pretty exciting, and even more exciting was riding in the car with my Aunt Mary driving!! Mom would tell my brothers and I that Aunt Mary drives a little fast, but don't worry, she knows what she is doing... oh boy... did she ever!! We were supposed to be looking at the Christmas lights as we were traveling downtown, but the kids in the back seat were holding on for dear life swaying back and forth as she swooped through traffic! We would all let out a deep breath when she would finally park so we could walk around looking at the big city Christmas lights all wide-eyed from all the colors on those tall buildings.

Those Christmases were so wonderful in those years. We would pack up the car with all the presents and off we would go to Massachusetts. Aunt Mary was a true culinary person, she was the director of the culinary department at Springfield College, and Uncle Walt was a professor there. Those holiday parties were full of food I had never tasted before. Everyone would dress up on Christmas Eve and the adults would have "toddies" from a big crystal bowl. It is amazing how I can still see my mother's holiday outfits that she wore that dad had bought for her specifically for the occasion. I can still see the fireplace and the orange overstuffed chairs in the entertainment area they had made in the lower part of their brick home. There would be a table full of food and as kids, we would take turns in going up to get more food to share. Aunt Mary sometimes would bring over a special plate of cookies or pastries she had made that looked too pretty to eat. What beautiful memories they are to reminisce over now as I wander through the memories of those Christmases.

Aunt Mary was one of the kindest people I have ever known, and her wisdom was astounding that she would share with me. I remember specifically that she never judged people and would say to me, "Never judge another person until you've walked a mile in their moccasins." I remember she even gave me a magnet of a moccasin for my refrigerator that had this saying on it. Aunt Mary had a deep respect for the Native American heritage. This saying is an American Indian proverb defining empathy. Empathy is essentially putting yourself in someone else's shoes and seeing the world from their point of view. This was so fitting for my Aunt Mary as she would share her stories of traveling around the world.

I remember one Christmas she and my mother dressed up in colorful silk clothes that Aunt Mary had brought home from Asia. She taught Mom how to put on the makeup that they wore and why they painted their face in a certain manner. Those gorgeous kimonos were so beautiful! They even put chop sticks in their hair as it was pulled up into a bun. Each time Aunt Mary and

Uncle Walt visited some country around the world, they would come and share the cuisine and customs that they learned from that country during their holiday visit.

Aunt Mary's teachings continued long after they moved to Arizona after they retired from the college. I remember the day they left Massachusetts and had everything in the back of a big box truck on their way across the country. I remember Dad getting that call from Uncle Walt telling him that as they were traveling down the highway, someone was flagging them down to tell them that the back of the box truck was on fire. Oh, how sad they were to realize that they had lost most of their belongings, and sadder still, was that they lost the antiques that were my father's and Aunt Mary's parents. Nana's furniture that she had given Aunt Mary was lost, furniture that had been passed down through generations. And I remember the conversation with Aunt Mary when mom and I went out to visit her. We went to the Grand Canyon, and there she told me that she had been robbed and the thieves had stolen the Swasey ring, a ring that had been passed down to the oldest daughter in the Swasey family for generations. She sat there in tears sharing with me that she felt so bad that I would never receive the family ring as the first daughter born in my generation.

Again, that strong sense of holding onto our heritage was present and passed down through the generations. The gift of listening to my Aunt Mary teaching me her principles and sharing her wisdom learned while traveling the world, and most importantly, her perseverance of staying true to herself. This is the same desire and gift that I try to share today with my children and grandchildren. All these experiences are imprints on my soul, they are part of my walk in Rose's Garden, my imprint of memories.

CHAPTER 8

NUGGETS, MEMORY STONES AMONGST THE STONE WALL OF MEMORIES

"Sometimes you will never know the value of a moment until it becomes a memory."
— *Theodore Geisel (Dr. Seuss)*

The gifts from our past become the nuggets of memories. I think of this as I reminisce about some experiences that I have had the blessing to be a part of in my career. There is one memory nugget that I think about every time I see "oysters" on a menu. Perplexed, are you?

You see there was this lady that I had the pleasure of knowing while managing a facility. She was as eccentric as they come and a "hoot" to talk to. She had traveled the world, and she and her husband were what you would call "tycoons." The beauty that I loved about her is that you would never know it just by sitting and having a conversation with her, as she had an old class of values about her. I remember one day when I went to visit her, and I asked her about the pictures on her wall. They were very beautiful and unique items that she held dear. There were not a lot of things but those that were there had deep memories for her to reflect upon. They represented things from around the world that reminded her of a time of joy and adventure, or as she would say, they involved ..."A lot of hard work!" But beyond her treasured items, she did have a tendency to clutter her room, and it wasn't the easiest to maneuver around in. The staff would come to me as she wouldn't let them in the room to clean. In her mind, it was never the right time to clean.

At this point in time, she was in her 90s, and she had that determination to "stand her ground" on what she wanted and when she wanted it. I would sit with her and go over the "why's" that we had to do certain things, especially around safety and cleanliness. She didn't like people to touch her things or her clothes. She had her clothes cleaned by a local dry-cleaning company that she had arranged to come weekly to pick them up. She also had some rules that people were to adhere to. She didn't want to be disturbed or have people come into her apartment until around 11 a.m. in the morning, and when you came, you needed to bring the newspaper, toast and her tea. She had her schedule, and we followed it. As it was, anyone with her stamina and wit, you really didn't have a choice in the matter!

But we came up with agreements that as a businesswoman, she understood that I had a business to run and that I, too, had rules I had to follow. Now mind you, she didn't like them, and at times would say to the staff, "I never agreed to any such thing!" And I would have to sit with her to review our agreement. Again, done as businesswomen to businesswoman. She would look up at me as I came through the door, "Oh, I see they called in the big guns." And she would smile that smile of hers. Just like the John Maxwell book, "Sometimes you win, and sometimes you learn," well she would push the envelope on the learning piece. She would say, "Anyone who has lived as long as she has deserved to do whatever they want." Well… who can argue with that statement? But as a licensed facility, I had to bring her back to the regulations, and reluctantly, she would agree. And what may you ask is this agreement talk all about…NOT SMOKING IN BED! It's true, she wanted to have her smokes. As a person who created programs around the desires of one's heart, this was a tough one for me. But when it came to safety, it wasn't an option for her to smoke in her bed anyway.

So, there we were, helping her get into her fur coat, and then helping her into her wheelchair to go for a stroll on the grounds so she could have her smoke. The staff would do this twice a day. The physician had convinced her to at least go down to twice a day for her smoking routine. She would give me her wave as the staff took her by my door to my office. That big smile of hers as she got her way to have her smokes, oh how I loved her determination!! She was a firecracker for sure!

It came to a point in her care when she was in hospice, and it was sad seeing her light fade. She didn't want to eat anymore, and we knew she was facing failure to thrive. I believe it was from a broken heart of losing her freedom and diminished stamina. Freedom refers to her health, as she was losing this battle in life. We wanted to find a "key" to help her light shine as she would like it to be. And then came the day that the Food and Beverage Director from our restaurant had an idea. He went to her room and they talked about food, discussing cuisine from around the world as this was one of her favorite joys. You see, our Food and Beverage Director was an amazing chef, and he had that gift and artistic ability to make the most amazing dishes. He knew this was one of her "keys" of life, her love of well-prepared food. And her most favorite food of all was fresh oysters. So, what did this chef do you ask? He arranged for a delivery of the freshest oysters from Boston to our facility, and he had them served daily to her in the half shell, on ice, with her favorite homemade cocktail sauce that he made with a garnish of fresh lemons.

This created a daily visit of food that sustained her until her body gave way to her disease. This heartfelt desire to bring a gift of hope, of eating again by boosting taste buds that she never thought would be possible, and igniting those memories from years past. She so looked forward to her visits with this chef and her oysters till the day she passed. What an amazing friendship and respect they had together all through the love of fine cuisine, and especially, a good cocktail sauce made with fresh horseradish and fresh lemons.

You see, the desires of one's heart can maintain a glimpse of hope and purpose. This nugget was the key that kept her desiring for tomorrow to come. It was actually part of her hospice program to ease her anxiety and to calm her soul with companionship and oysters. Memory stones of traveling the world, experiencing fine cuisine, and enjoying oysters with her husband helped her along her Walk in Rose's Garden, they now are part of her wall of memories.

A Wall of Memories Beside the Sea

CHAPTER 9

IMAGINE THE IMPOSSIBLE

"Logic will take you from A to B. Imagination
will take you everywhere."
— Albert Einstein

This quote is oh so true. I love the instinct of what Albert Einstein taught us around imagination. It is said that he was a curious, independent thinker from the time he was a young boy. He would visualize his ideas and create new thoughts around possibilities often going against popular opinions or traditions. He applied his "imagination" and demonstrated the enormous potential of a flexible mind.

During my career, I have been known to walk to the edge of the envelope of regulations and protocols in order to develop a different way of thinking and creating possibilities. I am no Einstein, but I believe we all have this capability. I have created many "memory paths" by walking through thoughts of origination and creativity in developing programs. I've had the gift of working with a group of people who wanted to find a kinder and gentler way to apply care, a care model that is holistic in nature and driven by the memories of joy, and even hardship, to hone in on a person's memory path in life. By creating this method of thinking, we developed many opportunities for university students to conduct fieldwork in our communities and create data to validate the findings.

One of my fondest memories includes a dynamic, vibrant soul that carried a light around her everywhere she went. When she walked into a room, her smile and her energy would light up that room. Everyone would turn their head to catch a glimpse of her as she went on her way. She was the guiding light for managing a university program of "who goes where," and what they would need when they got there. She was known as the glue that kept everyone on track of where they needed to go and what they needed to accomplish once they got there. She always said that she had a teacher, a mentor, who was a wise lady who taught her the "ropes" and with the gift of imagination that anything is possible. And even after this mentor, this beautiful soul passed from this earth, she still would feel her "pop in" as she would feel goosebumps and a presence that in no doubt was this soul confirming a new program or idea. We always used to say, "Boy, Darby would love this one!" As a new program was being created, the program would even get a big confirmation when "Darby's Magical Wand" that hung behind this lady's chair, would actually move... to give the idea a Darby blessing!! Oh, how we would laugh when this would happen, as we would say, "Well, this program is going to be fun!!"

This confirmation happened during a number of our program creations with the university. And a blessing it sure brought to those residents within the programs and to the students involved. It also brought an amazing acknowledgement in the world of quality care. Through these creations and documented outcomes that we captured through a data process, the programs earned recognition as a national quality award from the American Healthcare Association. We had the wonderful honor of being the recipient of a National Quality Award, and we went to Chicago to receive the award where we stayed in the famous Drake Hotel.

My husband and I had a room overlooking the southwestern shores of Lake Michigan. This small-town girl was in amazement at how grand the room was and how the facilities were so preserved in history. They even had a movie film being shot at the same time we were there, and we saw Robert DeNiro from a distance. What an experience this was... and then the awards evening day arrived. How grand it was as all the recipients were there to receive their award. Each of us had to line up by state to be given the Quality Award. I remember how nervous I was as I walked across the huge red and gold carpet where we walked diagonally across the room... but then what happened next made my night.

As I approached the opposite side of the carpet, out of the corner of my eye, I caught a glimpse of someone coming out from the crowd towards me. She was screaming with excitement, and I can still feel the "what the heck is happening" feeling as she came towards me. And then I saw her... it was my dear friend from the university who had traveled to the conference to see the recipients who they worked with receive their award. She ran out onto the carpet, grabbed me and swung me around with excitement. We grabbed each other's hands as we laughed and jumped up and down. The crowd cheered, joining in the celebration of the happiness being portrayed with pure joy.

So, here it was, my memory stone of pure joy and amazement was created. Darby's blessing and her wand of magical creativity was being recognized. Oh, how right Albert Einstein was... Imagination can take you everywhere!!!

CHAPTER 10

IT IS A BALANCE

"Life is like riding a bicycle. To keep your balance, you must keep moving."
—Albert Einstein

The journey in life is one that each one of us must travel in our own time. They say no two lives are parallel, and we each have our own lessons to learn along the way, but sometimes they sure walk a close timeline to life events! It has amazed me that after so many years of not seeing one of my classmates, to hear just how similar our life events have been.

I have a dear friend who I grew up with who I had not seen for 30 years. When we started sharing our lifes' journey, we found out that we were even pregnant at the same time and we had children of the same age. How strange it was that we were going through the exact same life event at the same time, and neither one of us knew it! Her persona had not changed one iota. She was the same bubbly personality that I always remembered. Another thing I noticed was that when she spoke, she sounded just like her mother! I would look at her, and in my mind, I would tip my head in amazement about how they sounded exactly the same. Oh, how its makes me smile as I have been told the same thing myself. One time, many years ago, I was walking through a store when a person who walked by me said, "Jean??" I turned to look at this man who was just standing there with this perplexed look on his face. He stood in amazement as he thought he was seeing my mom who had passed a number of years prior. Oh, how honored I was to think that my mom was so present in my image and mannerisms. I remember telling my friend that she acted and sounded like her mother and what it meant to her as well was exhibited as tears filled her eyes. We shared a gift treasured from years ago as a reflection of those we treasure most in life, our moms.

Those long memory stones of childhood were brewing up. We talked of all the times her mom would make us hot chocolate after playing in the winter snow. We laughed as we were remembering to how much snow we used to have, and she recalled the story of the neighbors dog that would come over to visit at her house. She talked about the fact that the snow banks were so tall that when the dog walked up to her house, he was standing on the bank looking through her second story window! He would stay there until she finally came out to the kitchen and see him at the window. She and her mom would laugh, and out the door she would go to play with this gorgeous shepard from neighbors next door. Imagine, snow up to the second story window!! We used to have some big snow storms in the 60's in Maine. We laughed reminiscing about going out on the snow banks and playing king of the mountain remembering which of our friends most often won and became king. Why we never broke a leg, I'll never know! It sure was a miracle and those angels had their work cut out for them keeping us safe! We were such rascals.

I remember one winter when the snow was deep and it blew right up and over the roof our neighbors garage. This garage was located right across from our family home, on what was rightly called, "windy corner," and windy it was!! The wind would come up from the fields below and sweep up the hill and then land right at that corner. So, you can imagine how tempting it was to sneak over to the garage, climb up on that snow drift, pull your sled up to the peek, and jump in the sled. Off you would go down the roof, and down the long hill to the fields below. Boy that was fun! Of course you had to time it just right as not to get caught, or so we thought. The funny thing was, that as children, we didn't think about that when you climbed a snow drift, it leaves quite a trail behind you from your sled and footsteps. So, as sneaky as we thought we were, we weren't really that successful in hiding it. But if we were lucky, the wind would be drifting, so, it would bury the evidence!!

We had many "rascal" days as kids in our tiny little town. We were gone from breakfast to supper on some days. In the summer, my friends would all come over to my house, (once dad left of course) and we would play basketball and ride our bikes playing cops and robbers. You see, we had a narrow sidewalk all around our house and that made for a great road to navigate and play on. On the corners, mom had lilac trees and big bushes that we would hide in as the "cops" tried to find us. All this fun could roll on throughout the day until around 4:30 in the afternoon when it was time for dad to come home. Then the neighborhood kids would scatter like cats! One day, when we were in the midst of an intense cops and robber episode, dad came home early. Oh my, the bikes were flying every which way finding a way to scoot back to their houses. But one young boy didn't make it. You see, he was actually hiding as a robber in one of our maple trees, and we all knew that John Swasey didn't like kids climbing in his maple trees! I didn't even know he was up there until I went into the living room to watch the news with dad. Dad had his black leather chair facing the big picture window looking out at his gorgeous maple tree. As I sat down on the couch next to where dad was sitting in his chair, I looked outside and

I squinted my eyes to try to make out what I was seeing in the tree. Oh Nooooo, this kid was standing in the maple tree leaning his back up against the trunk of the tree about 12 feet off the ground. I gasped under my breath. If I could see him, why wasn't dad seeing him!? I'm sure dad must have thought it strange as I sat right through the entire news broadcast that evening. In fact, I sat there long enough for it to become dark outside. That boy waited until dark so he could slip out of John Swasay's maple tree. Boy, that was a close one!!! I'll never forget how long that news program was that night waiting for the sun to set so that boy could get down from that tree.

Life is a balance. One little kilter, off balance, slip from that branch, and it would have ended quite differently for a few of us that day. If one takes a reflection of the meaning of "Life's Balance" you will find in encompasses eight dimensions. It is said that if you have even one of these eight dimensions out of balance, that over time, it can affect one's health, well-being and quality of life. What are these dimensions? The eight dimensions are; emotional, physical, occupational, social, spiritual, intellectual, environmental, and financial. It is said that by balancing these eight dimensions, it will provide holistic harmony to one's personal well-being. I have learned over the years that these dimensions are pillars to our memory stones in life. Each encompasses their own path and their own memory trail of experiences. If you think back through your life, and reflect on each of these dimensions, you will recognize how each one has affected another throughout your life. The balance of life through lessons learned are applied to achieve your next chapter in life. When reflecting upon your life story, consider each of these dimensions as you create your narrative story. These can act as a guidance of sort to reflect upon how each one worked with the other as you experienced life.

Lets take a look at what an "emotional journey" would look like. We all have one journey, and it has changed throughout our lives. Another way to think of it is in the aspect of emotional intelligence. This is how we perceive, use, understand, manage, and handle emotions., discerning between the different feelings of emotions within ourselves and others. It is a guide in thinking and behavior, discerning between different feelings and labeling them appropriately while we adjust emotions to adapt to the environment. Like with the boy who was standing in the tree waiting for the sun to set so he wouldn't get caught, this young boy was on overload with an emotional intelligence moment. He knew he had to adjust his emotions of staying in that tree until dark and used his environment to conceal himself from being seen in the tree. We all have these little moments that make up our memory walk, our staircase of experiences in life. In a Walk in Rose's Garden you will find it is filled with emotional intelligence moments. The fabric of life is entwined with all the emotions that maneuvered our next steps. These experiences, "memories," being written in a narrative story form will honor all those paths in life that we once took.

I have a book that sits by my favorite chair and I pick it up from time to time to read a poem or two, the title of the book is GRACE.

This one is written by Conor Obrest, a singer songwriter. He writes,

> *"I came upon a doctor who appeared in quite*
> *poor health. I said, 'There's nothing that I can*
> *do for you that you can't do for yourself.' He*
> *said, 'Oh yes you can. Just hold my hand I*
> *think that would help.' So, I sat with him for a*
> *while then I asked him how he felt. He said, 'I*
> *think I'm cured.'"*

The simple gesture of holding someone's hand without saying a word when all else is fading away is a gift beyond words. Being present in the moment and letting a person know that they are not alone is a gift that heals a lonely emotion or helps a moment of fear to fade away. That simple balance of life that calms a soul and gives hope that one is not alone. The touch of human kindness sometimes opens a door that someone may have been waiting to go through but didn't know how to navigate alone. I have experienced these moments in my career, and I can say that I have been truly blessed to have been chosen to help people walk through the gates of Rose's Garden. There is a peace that happens that one cannot explain in words, the sense of being amongst angels, and the struggles of one's walk diminishes.

A Walk in Rose's Garden reflects your own walk-in life, shared in a narrative story to assist one through those pathways in life. It is a gateway of sorts. Each path is unique to one's journey and special to the journey traveled. Take a moment to narrate your story with pictures of what your stepping stones may look like. Note the paths that reflect your story, and places that reflect your place of tranquility. Then narrate the sharing of your stories that you treasure and wish to have remembered. We have left pages at the end of this book for you to place some notes of reflection. Jot down those treasures in life and list your family and friends who you hold most dear.

These nuggets in life will start you down the path to narrate your story, so you can create your own *Walk in Rose's Garden: An Imprint of Your Memories.*

CHAPTER 11

AN IMPRINT OF OUR MEMORIES

"Memory is not just the imprint of the past time upon us; it is the keeper of what is meaningful for our deepest hopes and fears." —Rolo May

Rolo May was a master in gathering the stones of life and creating the path of revealed memories. In a write-up of his work, it states:

"I write for intelligent, open-minded, questioning, motivated laypeople. My writings are an endeavor to interpret to a larger public— that public of which is intelligently concerned with understanding themselves and the place and function of human beings in the world— what I have learned in my journeys into the

depth-psychology of human beings." [1]

He was a psychologist with a Ph.D. from Columbia University, and his writings were focused on helping people to understand their walk in life and the importance of their own existence. The simple way to view it is~we all matter. Our experiences in life matter, and the sharing of your story is a way of sharing a path of choices. It is not measured by how your path looks or what it encompasses, it is the fact that it is your story and yours alone. I have found out in life, that the experiences I have had oftentimes have been a moment of healing for another who may be experiencing a similar experience. Having a person who can "see" the feelings and experience the "unknowns" that one feels when facing a life event can be like an angel sent to sit beside you and a "knowing" of a similar experience.

I remember so vividly a moment in my childhood when I was playing softball in high school. We had an amazing team, and we were climbing our way up to the state championship. I can remember one game that I was pitching when the umpire came up to me after the game and said, "That was the most exciting game I have ever called, to think you pitched a no-hitter!" I remember looking at him in amazement as I was just excited that we had won the game, and we were on our way to the championship. You see, to him, it was a rare opportunity to umpire a no-hitter. To me, it was a celebration of a team's win. I often reflect on it now as listen to my brother share the stories of his granddaughters playing softball and one of them pitching multiple no-hitters. To see all three of his granddaughters play through pictures celebrating as the team who won the state championship is so exciting. Oh, how exciting for them to win the championship together, they will remember that moment for a lifetime!!

1   *Reflections and Commentary by Rollo May in The Psychology of Rollo May by Clement Reeves, 1977*

I was so glad I had a coach with that same philosophy. She taught us to sync with one another, to use each other's strengths to build a powerhouse team. This coach played a very important part in my life. She was tough, but she was fair. I'll never forget the day that I was getting ready to play the championship game, and we were all pumped up, just playing around and warming up before the game. We were out there throwing balls from base to base and our catcher, with an arm of steel and a bat like Paul Bunyan, was hitting us balls to warm us up. I had gone out to play second base fooling around and throwing the balls hard, back and forth to my teammates when a ball was hit up the middle. I ran to give the ball a "swoop" with my glove, and down I went as I caught my toe on the second base bag. When I landed, I knew I was in trouble. I landed on my upper shoulder, my collarbone area and I heard a snap. I felt a little faint, but I stood up determined to shake it off as the coach started to come out to the field. I shook her back and said I was fine, not moving my left arm from my body. We all gathered to cheer our chant to victory and out to the mound I went. I stood there for a second, and then I motioned for the catcher, my longtime friend and softball catcher right up through childhood, to come out to the mound. She pulled back her mask and jogged out to the mound. I said to her…"Um, don't throw the ball so hard back to me okay?" She just stared at me and said, "What's up?" I said, "Just don't, okay?" She pulled down her mask and back to home plate she went. So, I took the ball and threw it towards home plate for the first pitch. I thought I was going to throw up, it hurt so bad. And then she threw the ball back to the mitt in my left hand…man, did that hurt. I pitched three balls, and then the coach raised her hand to the umpire. Tears were streaming down my face as she took that long walk towards the mound. She said to me, "So, are you done? Have you had enough?" She knew I had to try. She knew that if I didn't, I would have always wondered whether I would have been able to do it. And then she waved the first base player over to the mound and held me as we went back to the sidelines. She said, "You ready to go to the hospital? You broke it didn't you?" I told her I may have. I felt so bad as I felt as though I was letting everyone down.

It was one of the hardest moments of my life as a child to leave that game that day. And yes, I did break it, and my pitching was never the same after that healed. I was still able to throw curve balls, but they didn't have the speed they had before. Life changed from that moment on. I will always be grateful for the opportunity to have been coached by this wonderful lady. She taught us more than just softball through those years, she showed us how to be a team. She taught us how to recognize our strengths and our weaknesses so we would become a well-oiled machine. But she also taught us another major message. She taught us the ability to listen and to embrace the wisdom of others. If I had only listened to her that day and gone and warmed up pitching as she had asked me to do, I wouldn't have broken my collarbone.

That day was a big turning point in my life, more than anyone and even myself could ever have imagined. You see, breaking my collarbone that day was the third time that I had broken my collarbone on that same side. Over the years, this created a tremendous shift in my life that I'm still dealing with today. That was a pivotal moment in my life realizing that if I had only listened, things may have been different. I shared with you earlier in the book a stone pathway that took a large diversion to one side. This shift led to a different lifestyle that I'm living today. By the weakening of the muscles on my neck from the three broken collar bone incidents, in the same area, it weakened the muscle that goes up behind my ear on my left side. My path now is forever changed. It has left me with a condition called thoracic outlet syndrome. This is a condition that affects circulation to my left arm and across my chest, which limits me in how I do things today. I have learned to adapt to my new reality of not being able to do certain things, or to be able to lift things the way I used to.

That choice, in that moment, at that game, forever changed my path. When I saw the vision of this rock and how it reflects upon my own life, I knew this was part of my walk and Rose's Garden. Please note in the image of this picture, that the path continues, but it just looks different than what it would've looked before this accident happened. Circumstances in life doesn't mean that we stop living, it just means that we change the way we live. Remember, as Albert Einstein would say, "Life is like riding a bicycle. To keep your balance, you must keep moving."

But, reflecting back, if it hadn't been for that choice that day, I may not have had such a desire to help people be successful, or to be able to explore their potential as intently as I do today. By experiencing the feeling that I let everybody down in that game that day, it instilled in me a deep desire, and a will to help others succeed. It has been a true passion in my life and all through my healthcare career. Whether it was to help a resident to do something they never thought they were able to do again, or to help a staff member who couldn't imagine becoming a certified nursing assistant become one. This was done by applying for a grant with the State, and we were able to send five staff members to school to further their education, and some of them have become nurses. Some experiences change our course in life, and some changes can bring growth. Socrates said, "The secret of change is to focus all of your energy, not on the fighting the old, but on building the new." Change created a new path for you to experience and at times equips us with what we may need in our next chapter of life. That imprint, of that particular memory, helps us to take the next step, and sometimes helps us to help others through a similar experience.

In reflecting upon your memory stones, consider those pillars of life balance. We all have had to navigate them to keep life moving, they encompass our tapestry of life.

LIFE'S BALANCE PILLARS: the emotional path (a marriage, a birth of a child, or a loss of loved one), the physical path in life (our journey with health, like my collarbone incident), our occupational path (like my healthcare career or raising children), the social path (what activities you like to do, like mine is walking in the forest and enjoying time with my children, grandchildren, family and friends, playing with my dog Sasha and my horse Maverick), our spiritual journey (where you find your peace, your religion or your beliefs, like my mother's angels whispering in my ear that helps me through life), the intellectual path (it may be your educational journey or the type of books you like to read), our environmental path (where we have lived and/or traveled in our life or even your place of comfort, a rural setting or a city, or even just the smell of fresh hay in a barn), and you may want to share **your financial journey** of how you made it through life on a shoestring by being a hard worker to keep food on the table. These all encompass our life balance story.

We all have had these journeys, and we navigated them as best we could with what we had at the time and to the best of our ability. The memory path is not that of shame, or the 'ole shoulda, coulda, woulda's in life, it is a reflection of our journey; the good, the bad or otherwise. Each turn in the path has led to the next journey. It is looking at life through your lenses.

Sharing your Walk in Rose's Garden is not measured on what is included in your life's journey. It doesn't matter if you have had children or have not had children. It doesn't matter if you're a college graduate or even if you finished school. What matters is the experiences you had that are yours in life. It is embracing your own journey and sharing the life story that only you can tell. It can be done through pictures of your life in a scrap book with narrative notes below the pictures. Remember to add pictures where you experience tranquility and a vision of what your "Memory Stones" of life might look like. Through the pages of this book, you have embarked upon my reflections of life. My place of tranquility was sitting by a babbling brook in the midst of the western mountains of Maine. The cover of this book reflects my "Walk" through life. They reflect my memory stones of the path I walked throughout my life's journey.

All of these imprints in life can reveal a deeper understanding of your life, and your experiences in life. Embrace your journey and share the path traveled. I feel it is important for generations to come to learn about the life you lived, and it may help someone who is walking a similar path. Share your path taken so those near and dear at heart can learn about your joys, heartaches, accomplishments and struggles so all this information doesn't disappear once we have left this earth. Who knows, it may even offer a "hand-up" to someone needing encouragement to embrace their day.

CHAPTER 12

THE GIFT OF THE STORY, THE MEMORY STONES OF LIFE

"There is life in a stone. Any stone that sits in a field or lies on a beach takes on the memory of that place. You can feel that stones have witnessed so many things."
—Andy Goldsworthy

Andy Goldsworthy is an English sculpturer and photographer with a deep respect for nature. The picture on the next page, *The Storm King Wall*, spans over 500 acres. Storm King Art Center is home to the country's largest collection of contemporary outdoor sculpture. This photo was taken by Christian Purple courtesy of Shutterstock.

Goldsworthy's art is crafted from natural resources like rocks, ice, and leaves documented with the passing of time, and he captures this through his photography. His artistic process is a "collaboration with nature." His process requires patience and flexibility, in most instances, using only his hands as his primary tools of choice. Embracing the philosophy of each stone has a life of its own, a reflection of history, and honors the gift of nature.

There are other teachings that I found relating to the memory stones of life. There is a biblical precedent of laying stones through biblical history. It is said this is done as a remembrance of what the good Lord has done for us, a remembrance of our life's journey. There are three specific stories that reference the setting of memory stones. One was to memorialize a powerful vision as not to forget what God had given Jacob in Genesis 28:10-22. Another was a marker of miraculous works when the Israelites crossed the Jordan River, and the 12 stones of Jordan reminds us of God's love in Joshua 4:1-8. And there is one that represents the stone of help, of God's grace in our lives in 1 Samuel 7:7-12. It is said that these stones represent a way to reflect on the gifts that God has bestowed upon us so that our faith did not falter and would be renewed.

Our memory stones of life are unique to our life's experiences. In our reflection of life, it is amazing how this correlates to the three precedents found in the Bible. The remembrance of life has given us experiences, the love we have encountered along the way, and the grace we received along our journey. These are all entwined in our life journey.

By knowing someone's life story, I have witnessed watching their respirations slow down and seen the comfort on their faces just by them hearing the words of someone "knowing" their path. It has been known for some time that these memory stones of life are essential as a tool to a gateway for those journeying through life's path.

In our world today, many times, people are left on their own to navigate the road of someone's final transitions in this life. With the healthcare challenges that we are faced with since 2020, when the world changed from the effects of COVID, the healthcare system is struggling. The lack of nurses, caregivers, and other disciplines is being felt from hospitals to homecare. Having the assistance that one may need has become a challenge. Being informed of the right information, being informed of the choices that one may have available to them, and where to get it, seems to be limited or not communicated as the tools they could be. This is the burden that healthcare is faced with, and there needs to be a way, a resource that helps one navigate this journey called life.

When we had our hospice program in the assisted living facilities that I managed, we focused on all three categories of hospice services. *Routine home care, Continuous Care*, which is for an acute symptoms management at home by hospice staff 24 hours a day to avoid hospitalization, and *Respite Care* which is a benefit of five consecutive days of pain and symptom management typically in the final stages of life. What I have found with people who I know who were in need of these hospice services for their loved one, is that the services that we used to provide, as the known categories of hospice care, were not discussed. I have been amazed that this was not part of the hospice service plan. This type of assistance, especially in a home setting, is crucial, and it is a Medicare benefit through hospice.

Being informed is a right that we all have in order to be able to make sound choices. When we are not informed, then we are not working with all the information to help us navigate the path before us. Hospice is an important program that is there to assist the caregiver along with the patient. The gift I had of helping those in their final journey in life in the buildings I managed was the gift of knowing their walk in Rose's Garden through their life stories. Knowing their life stories and assisting in the transition of honoring their journey, all encompassed the act of supporting the families. All these acts were supported through the hospice agency staff along with our staff in the facility.

When living in an assisted living facility in Maine, it is considered the resident's home, and in our setting, we were able to offer an apartment with all their personal belongings set around them. Having the hospice services available to us to support the staff and the families allowed us to utilize the categories of hospice care that were available through the Medicare hospice benefit. This meant that we could offer the hospice care in A Walk in Rose's Garden. Hospice nurses would be assigned to the resident, and they were the support staff to help us care for the resident. When the resident was transitioning and we needed additional support for the family and our staff, they would assess the need for respite care service for symptom and pain control and/or continuous care level of care. This may have been for a 24-hour period of that hospice nurse being by the residents side, or the five-day support of respite care for those situations that were more complex. This would relieve care giver exhaustion that the family may have been experiencing, it would support the care team within the facility, and it was that special care need service of an expert in hospice care for added comfort measures for the resident.

I have heard that the home care hospice experiences have been a challenge due to lack of staffing and especially the aspects of those living in a rural setting. Knowing a kinder way to support those who are going through this final transitioning as we experienced in the Walk in Rose's Garden, with the purpose of delivering this service in their own home as a goal, it weighs heavy on my heart to the state of the care model and the challenges expressed today. Knowing that rules that govern these services change and that "due process" is adopted from experiences that went awry, I question if these instances resulted in a change in services available in a home setting today.

I've always thought of this vision when describing the care needs of a person. If we took the view of the Christmas tree and turned it upside down and placed all the needs of that person inside utilizing all the tools and programs available to us, then the final plan would drip on the person in need of all the services and support that we know to exist. Wouldn't that be a kinder approach and honor their journey? We would also want to add the discipline of Occupational Therapy as they focus on the patient's life story as a pivotal part of their care.

When looking up the definition around Occupational Therapy as part of hospice services, this is what it says:

> *Occupational therapy is a vital part of hospice.*
> *Therapists play an integral role in hospice care*
> *teams through the identification of life roles*
> *and activities that provide some meaning to*
> *patients, all while addressing barriers that may*
> *exist when performing such activities.*

As part of my research around Occupational Therapy and hospice. I found this information from the National Library of Medicine, NIH. This document, *Addressing the Gap: Occupational Therapy in Hospice Care*, validates that Occupational Therapy helps instill the dignity that everyone should experience during end of life. This is the link to the white paper, and I have included a snip of the material for you to see. https://www.ncbi.nlm.nih.gov/pmc/articles/PMC8192430/

Addressing the Gap: Occupational Therapy in Hospice Care

Emily Mueller,[a] Paul Arthur,[b,c] Mack Ivy,[d] Loree Pryor,[a] Amber Armstead,[a] and Chih-Ying Li[a,*]

▸ Author information ▸ Copyright and License information   Disclaimer

The publisher's final edited version of this article is available at Occup Ther Health Care

Abstract   Go to: ▸

Patients receiving hospice care have a host of occupational challenges, though few are being seen in occupational therapy for treatment. Occupational therapy can help those receiving hospice care live with dignity before death. Data retrieved from the National Home and Hospice Care Survey were analyzed using independent t-tests, Wilcoxon rank-sum tests, Chi-square tests and logistic regressions. Only 10.6% of the participants received occupational therapy. Patients who received occupational therapy were significantly older and had shorter lengths of hospice care service compared to their counterparts. Over 85% of the patients needed assistance with at least one task of activity of daily living (ADL). Findings suggested a need to increase occupational therapy workforce in hospice care and advocate the value of occupational therapy services in hospice settings.

Keywords: occupational therapy, hospice, palliative, quality of life

Hospice care is a benefit for individuals certified to be terminally ill with a medical prognosis including a life expectancy of six months or less, should the illness run its traditional course (Centers for Medicare & Medicaid Services [CMS], 2018). Occupational therapy is one of the hospice care services that can assist the patients to maintain independence in meaningful activities of daily living and functional skills (CMS, 2018, section 40.1.8). CMS indicates that occupational therapy, along with other services such as physical therapy and speech-language therapy, must be provided in hospice settings, either directly or arranged, to address and meet the patient or family's needs (CMS, 2018, section 40.5). To date, the number of individuals needing hospice care services has grown to nearly 20 million worldwide. However, only 14% of those individuals actually receive the end of life care they need (Von Post & Wagman, 2019).

It amazes me that only 14% of people actually receive the benefit and care that one is entitled to. And the walk between the definition of Occupational Therapy as hospice services mirror the program we shared within A Walk in Rose's Garden. I feel it is a missed opportunity if people are not given this option while receiving hospice services.

This Occupational Therapy hospice service is the epitome of A Walk in Rose's Garden's focus. It is the summary access to the life story. They identify the "memory stones of life" that express the love, the vision, and the grace of their path traveled. They can assist helping the person identify the "vision" of remembrance as one journeys through their final days in life. The occupational therapist may assist in identifying the "view" or the meaning of the person's experiences, the road traveled throughout their life. They can help identify the barriers that may exist, like in the stories of the gentleman who conducted ops in WWII and the lady who escaped Europe with her sister, and the imprints these experiences left in their life's journey. The purpose of the occupational therapist is to act as the gentle hand, holding the hand of another, to show compassion and respect for a life lived with dignity, compassion, and honor. To assist and offer a balance of a life lived, they can help with the struggles of loneliness, isolation, abandonment, detachment from the world, fear, and loss of control.

I was encouraged to read a program that resembles the Walk in Rose's Garden called Storii. You can find the concept at Storii.com, and this is an excerpt from their website.

> *When someone reaches the end of their life, they naturally reflect on their past. Erikson's developmental theory stresses the importance of reminiscing to the psychological health of an individual. He describes a person's last developmental task as the reworking of one's past. That last task is to reach acceptance of what one's life was, and for what someone has been. Erikson phrased it as: "to be--through having been."*
>
> *Reminiscence (i.e., the ace or process of recalling past events or experiences) and its therapeutic proclivities has garnered much attention within the healthcare world in recent years. This is especially true for the dementia and end-of-life care fields. Life Story or Legacy Work and Ethical Wills are other valued activities that fall under the umbrella term of Reminiscence. Each of these hold particular importance in hospice and palliative care.*

YES! There is support out there, and there are programs and services available for people, and they embrace the gift of honoring a life lived. I find that the barrier still exists in that people are not familiar with "how to navigate the process," especially during times of heartache and being all consumed with the loss before them.

By giving people an informed choice and educating them about the services being offered as entitled benefits, the result would be a service of programs to help one honor their life story.

I've always appreciated this quote shared by John Maxwell where he values this message from his mentor. He wrote, "When opportunity comes, it's too late to prepare." These words were said by John Wooden, and oh how true they are. John Robert Wooden was an American basketball coach who won 10 National Collegiate Athletic Association's national championships in a 12-year period for the UCLA Bruins. In his method of coaching, his philosophy was, *He simply taught his teams to try to prepare themselves to the best of their ability to be the best they could be, and the result would take care of itself.*"

So, there it is... simply said. To prepare ourselves to the best of our ability to be the best we can be. To be informed of what is available to us and to set it into motion, to put it into play, as to what I imagine John Wooden would say. It isn't complicated, it isn't something that is unachievable, it is simply a focus of helping oneself to achieve the best they could be.

So, how does this correlate to A Walk in Rose's Garden: An Imprint of our Memories, you ask? It is the mindset of caring for oneself by achieving the gift of recording one's life story. The imprints of all those paths traveled and treasured as the reflection of one's past. As Erikson phrased it, "to be—through having been." A glimpse of history, your history, that can be shared through generations like the books I have the gift to hold of my great, great, great grandfathers. To see the pen from the hand that I can only imagine holding is a priceless gift. It may be in a book form or pages shared in a journal, but it all is a treasure to hold, a reflection of life once lived. It also becomes tools and whispers of hope when navigating one's final steps on earth. It is a window of time being shared from your own perspective, and it can offer assistance to those who will be caring for you.

My hope is that this book inspires people to ponder such thoughts and reflect upon the journey of their life. The true gift shared is the visions that you had, the experiences and memories you have had, and the barriers that you may have encountered along the way. These are the reflections of your story.

The "Walk" within Rose's garden are the memory stones of life. Some of the stones are placed just lying on the surface, and some stones lie deep down within the ground, but they all encompass your life. To share the vision of what your path may look like, a path of tranquility, hope, and joy, a place that aluminates your place of refuge and of peace is needed.

It is a place shared like this, a vision of your Walk in Rose's Garden, that once known and shared, can be referred to as we travel beyond the bend in the path of life. It is as an act of giving comfort.

How do you start one you may ask. There is no perfect rule. It is the act of "starting the journey" that is important. To have a beginner's mindset. Erwin G. Hall shared, "An open mind is the beginning of self-discovery and growth. We can't learn anything new until we can admit that we don't already know everything." What do all beginners have in common? John Maxwell shares… "They know they don't know it all." He shares these three points to think about.

1. Everyone has something to teach me.

2. Every day I have something to learn.

3. Every time I learn something, I benefit.

My Place of Tranquility

He shares these intentionally asked questions and listens to the guidance before him. By using this mindset, you can achieve your goals. Each day is another opportunity to learn, to grow as a person no matter what your age may be. It is all an act of self-discovery as a reflection of your life lived within your story of a Walk in Rose's Garden.

So, plant a seed and start down the path of reminiscence, the act or process of recalling past events and experiences. Jot down the tools that you learned through these pages of how you can share your life story. Remember that you are not alone when facing an unknown future, that there are supports and systems, benefits and programs out there to be of support to you and to those you love. Educate yourself and learn ways that bring these three things value in your life... your vision of the place of tranquility, the love that is entwined within our memories, and the faith that by sharing these memory stones, it will bring refuge to those you love. This is a journey we all will take, and it will be that of a kinder nature. It will be valued and honored as it should be.

Remember these words, "Remember, it's the finish, not the start, that counts most in life." From *Humility: The Spirit of Learning* by John Maxwell.

We have placed blank pages at the end of this book for you to reference and record pieces of your Walk in Rose's Garden. You can reflect back to the different chapters to collect ideas on what you would like to record as your memory stones of life. Remember to include those benefit rights you want for yourself to be sure they are available. Remember to have questions written, a list of things that would be helpful while you are in your journey along life's path. Remember to share your joys, and your fondest memories as windows of the soul so they can be treasured. And share special songs, poems, and books that feed your soul as a reference to help others navigate this path.

In the next chapter, I will share one of mine....

Reflect Upon Your Journey ... Honor Your Path in Life

CHAPTER 13

ONE'S LIFE WORK

"Poems of simple faith."
—a note from a friend

I once had a book show up that I truly treasure. I refer to this as showing up, as that has been my experience through life. Things show up in the pivotal moment they were needed. This book was written in 1888 called, *The Poets of Maine: A Collection of Specimens Poems From Over Four Hundred Verse-Makers of the Pine-Tree State.* It was compiled by George Bancroft Griffith in Portland, Maine. It is a gorgeous, thick bound, forest green book with gold inlay letters and the pages are trimmed with gold.

This book sat in my office, and from time to time, residents, family members, and others would ask to look at or borrow it as it had something to share with them. There was this one man with a gentle soul who came to visit his wife every single day. If he couldn't drive, he would walk in order to have a moment with the love of his life. Mind you, he was in his late 80s to early 90s. I still have the note he left me after taking the book to read at home for a few days. He simply wrote, *"Karen, Thank you, poems of simple faith, surprising nothing of the war."* With a smiley face as a signature.

I never really took notice to the reference of the word "war" as I am now, and I see now that he may have been referring to one of these four wars. The War of 1812, the Mexican-American War, the Civil War, and the Spanish American War. Well, no wonder he referenced that point! You would have to figure that he was born in the early 1900s, and his parents must have had many conversations around the stories of that era. Life is a perspective, his was different than mine as he lived in a different era. As I traveled through the pages of the book, I saw the poems of simple faith along with names of towns and places that I had heard of around the state of Maine.

There was one particular poem that truly stood out to me. To this day, it is one that I still read from time to time. This poem was written by Caroline Fletcher Dole. She was born in Nor-ridgewock, Maine in July of 1817. She married a pastor of the First Congregational church, Nathan Dole from Brewer, Maine. It is noted that she was editor of missionary periodicals in the Missionary House in Boston. This is the poem:

Work for Christ

"What can I do for the Master?" I said in sadness one day; "I should work much better and faster, for life is fleeting aways."

I thought of the poor, marred tissue, wrought for his critical eye; and I prayed for faire issue, of the shuttle yet to fly.

Tears dinned my eye, and fell thicker, but I needed, for avail, a faith that should burn and not flicker, a love that should never fail.

"What shall I do for the Master?" Again to myself I said; "I must use much better and faster the rest of life's precious thread."

And a small, wan child now waited, for my aid, outside the door, like a fluttering bird, belated, and finding its nest no more.

Then shortly, a dusky figure peered in, on my startled sight; and he asked, with sad, pleading gesture, for the Way, the Truth, the Light.

But ere I applied my lesson, Lo! Down the old shaded street, (Did I dream?) a vast procession came onward, with weary feet.

I could never paint it truly, with skillfullest painter's brush, or portray the dark shadows duly, I saw in that twilight's hush.

What a mass of upturned faces, so wild, and haggard, and low; bearing plainly the fearful traces of sin, and disease, and woe!

Ah me! How it swelled and lengthened! "Will it never end?" I said; but at eve it was only strengthened, and I heard its heavy tread.

"See, here is work!" Said the Master, "Think you it can bear delay? Yes, rise and work better and faster, the rest of life's fleeting day."

"Inasmuch as for these ye labor, I accept it as to me; in thy poor and thy needy neighbor, they Lord, and the Master see?"

Then I rose, and wrought in life's tissue, some fair, bright colors for these; and light and joy was the issue, and my Lord I sought to please.

And I said, "O dearest Master, Strengthen thy laborer's hands, to work the better and faster, seeing thy blessed commands."

So, this has been my compass, that I take notice of everything and everyone that enters my path of life. I strive to be the best that I can be in what I attempt to do as to take heed and listen to the lessons that are before me. Each encounter has brought meaning, in one form or another, and has made me a better person. Keeping eyes forward and noticing the things around me, the way my father taught me as a child walking through the woods. Embracing each encounter as a lesson learned and acknowledging it as the gift that it truly is.

So, these lessons learned and the sharing of stories of those who I have taken with me through life, have become my template to my Walk in Rose's Garden.

When you think of me, you will find me sitting on a banks of a crystal clear brook, listening to the birds amongst the hemlock and cedar trees, with the smell of leaves and the rays of sunshine coming down creating orbs of angels in beautiful colors. I will be gazing upon my path, reminiscing of my memory stones, my pathway in life, and reflecting upon my visions, my loves, and my faith that supported me through my travels. I see my path to get there as a rock staircase covered with moss with rocks of all sizes and dimensions representing my depth of memories and whimsical days.

The cover of this book is my pathway that I imagine taking to the stream. There I will reflect upon my memories of years past. This is only part of my vision of tranquility, as my journey to get there starts with me walking along a stone wall in a field on the hillside of the mountain with a clear blue sky. As I amble along towards my rock staircase, you will find me walking with the roaming horses that are feeding upon the rich green grass in the fields. I will wave to all of those who I hold dear as I travel up my staircase to my place of refuge where my dreams are gathered and my memories live forever more.

My tapestry in life from the back of my canvas may look quite messy and make no sense at all, but when you turn it around, this narrative will be the vision that will be before you. Life's imperfections are always our lessons, and they create the wisdom that we use throughout life's journey.

I remember one time when I had this clear vision that appeared in front of me. It was an image that I could see as clear as a bell. In the vision was an image of me, and in my hand, I had a tiny rock hammer. There was this large wall in front of me, and I couldn't see my way around it. Then, I could see myself using the little rock hammer, swinging it swing after swing hitting the rock wall. I made a tiny hole to where I could see a bright light coming through. I noticed the feeling I had of courage and determination as I kept swinging the rock hammer. This feeling stayed with me as long as I didn't look down at all the chips on the ground, and I focused on the light in the wall. And then I heard these words. "Keep swinging your hammer and focus on that small hole where you see the bright light coming through. This hole was created by all your determination and perseverance you endured through life."

With every swing of faith, I was getting to a brighter place of comfort, surety, and peace. But there was something else that I noticed that happened. Every time I looked down at the chips I hammered off the wall, I would feel a sense of being anxious, unsure, and hopelessly lost. I heard again, "When you take your eyes off the light, and you look down, you are looking at all the doubts and failures that you have worked hard to learn from. So, lift your head, and pick up your hammer, and fix your eyes on the light, because no matter how small of a mark you make, you are growing stronger. Keep swinging with your efforts of faith." So, look up my friends and grab your hammer and start swinging at that wall. You can create your Walk in Rose's Garden, to share your imprints of memories.

"Look at a stone cutter hammering away at his rock, perhaps a hundred times without as much as a crack showing in it. Yet at the hundred-and-first blow it will split in two, and I know it was not the last blow that did it, but all that had gone before.
—Jacob A. Riis

I have mentioned songs that reflect your life as a way of sharing your heart and your Walk in Rose's Garden. This song by Kutless is such a reflection of what I have experienced in life. Here are the lyrics:

What Faith Can Do

Everybody falls sometimes
Gotta find the strength to rise
From the ashes and make a new beginning.
Anyone can feel the ache
You think it's more than you can take
But you're stronger, stronger than you know.

Don't you give up now
The sun will soon be shining,
You gotta face the clouds
To find the silver lining.

I've seen dreams that move the mountains
Hope that doesn't ever end
Even when the sky is falling.
I've seen miracles just happen
Silent prayers get answered,
Broken hearts become brand new,
That's what faith can do.

It doesn't matter what you've heard
Impossible is not a word,
It's just a reason for someone not to try.
Everybody's scared to death
When they decide to take that step
Out on the water,
But it'll be alright.

Life is so much more
Than what your eyes are seeing,

You will find your way
If you keep believing.

I've seen dreams that move the mountains
Hope that doesn't ever end
Even when the sky is falling.
I've seen miracles just happen
Silent prayers get answered,
Broken hearts become brand new,
That's what faith can do.

Overcome the odds
When you don't have a chance
(That's what faith can do)
When the world says you can't
It'll tell you that you can.
I've seen dreams that move the mountains
Hope that doesn't ever end
Even when the sky is falling.
I've seen miracles just happen
Silent prayers get answered,
Broken hearts become brand new,
That's what faith can do
That's what faith can do.

Even if you fall sometimes
You will have the strength to rise.

A Beautiful Orb Over Sebago Lake

"MY STORY", *A Story by a Friend*

I have had a lot of careers in my life: mother of three, grand-mother of five, a National Ski Patroller in Vermont, a Constable on the Mounted Police in Massachusetts, and a Mounted Search and Rescue Volunteer. My career as a Massage Therapist had its beginnings as a child...it just took me awhile to begin it. When our grandmother would visit, I would hop in her bed, and she would lovingly rub my back. To this day, I can be stopped in my tracks if my back is being rubbed.

I saw clients in many places in Massachusetts. One was with developmentally disabled people in their homes or in the hospital. Another was a massage group where I eventually honed my skills to provide gentle relief in the areas of prenatal/postpartum and oncology. A third place was a non-profit organization that provides relief, counseling, and support to oncology patients and their caregivers.

Bonnie was one of my very favorite clients. Her life history was deep and rich with travel and a love of life. At 80, her life changed with the addition of a male friend, and she would beam when re-telling the details of the trips that they were taking together. She had cancer and had recovered from it, but, as with all who have recovered, it was important to see a massage therapist with on-cology training to ensure that no problems arose from too much pressure in particular areas during the massage.

Just prior to the beginning of COVID, Bonnie was having trouble driving and walking. I would take my table to her home and give her massages. Conversation flowed while she relaxed. It was just a continuation of a wonderful friendship.

COVID happened, and Bonnie found herself becoming bedrid-den. The diagnosis was terminal, and Hospice became a part of her life. The United States had shut down on March 13, 2020; no one was going anywhere nor seeing anyone. But Bonnie called me on March 27, 2020, and she asked me to come by, to give her a massage, and to say goodbye. What else could I do?

Gowned in my own version of a HAZMAT suit (a black trash bag, latex gloves, two face masks, safety glasses and a shower cap), I went to her home where her three daughters were in residence. They welcomed me warmly (and laughingly at my outfit) and showed me to her room. She was as charming and funny as ever, and so glad to see me. It brings tears to my eyes even today as I think of my friend, my client.

As it turned out, Bonnie comforted me as much as I was providing comfort to her. Her love of life, her love of her family, her decision to let go, and her strength helped not just this massage therapist, but all her friends and family.

I have been working at a non-profit organization for the past 10 years and have been providing oncology massage for their clients. I have met some incredible people whose life stories are carried in my heart. These wonderful people have faced cancer, have fought it, and won. And there is a population of people who have made the decision to complete their lives with a smile and enjoy life right now with chocolate ice cream for breakfast. Why not?

JANICE PETERMAN, LMT

"There are always angels amongst us"

*It has always amazed me that everywhere I go
I find a white feather lying on the ground. It
is even more amazing that I find them when I
swim back in from the lake...as they are waiting
for me on top of the water as I come close to the
shore.
These white feathers make me smile as I have
had them "show up" as a reminder of all the
times my mother told me..."Pay attention, there
may be angels close by, as they drop a feather to
show me they are near....my guardian angels.*

These stories and tapestry portrayed of my own life is here to help you to reflect upon your own life and reminisce of your own stories, your dreams, your visions, and to honor the gift of the life you have lived.

It is now time for you to create your...

"A Walk in Rose's Garden,
The Stepping Stones of **YOUR** Life."

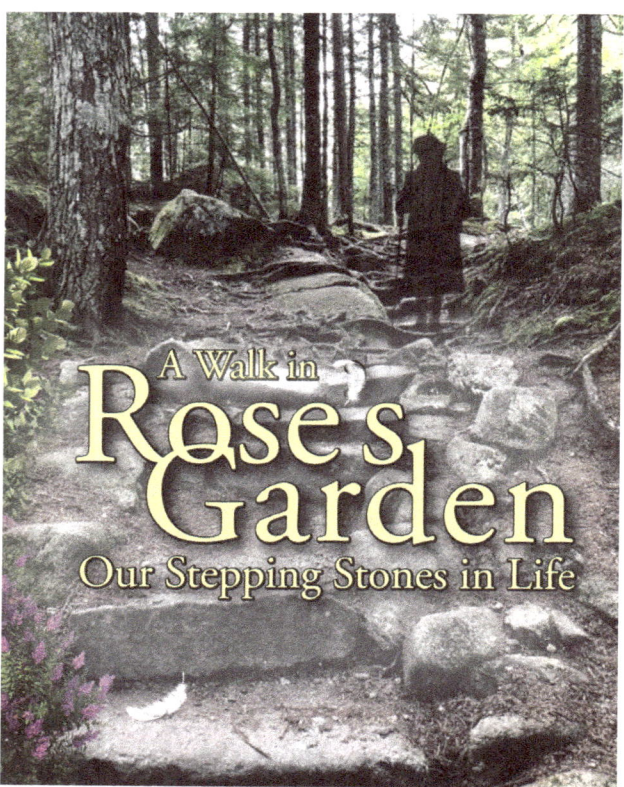

This Is My Walk in Rose's Garden

NAME: _____

MY FAMILY TREE

A NARRATIVE OF MY VISION

A NARRATIVE OF MY MEMORIES

A NARRATIVE OF MY MEMORIES

A PHOTO OF MY VISION

"Life Story" samples can be downloaded from a website where you can print out copies to start your own narrative story.

You can find it at this link:
https://www.legacyproject.org/activities/lifestory.pdf

Here is the site of benefits explanations in hospice.
https://www.medicare.gov/care-compare/resources/hospice/levels-of-care

REFERENCES

- medicare.gov for research
- legacyproject.org for Life Story material
- ncibi.hih.nih.gov statistics
- storii.com Life Story material
- eternalwall.org Life Story material
- Jacob.riis Quotes
- afar.com Storm King Wall
- Botanical Gardens of Maine
- Ralph Waldo Emerson Quote
- John C. Maxwell-The Maxwell Daily Reader, Developing the Leader within You, Humility: The Spirit of Learning
- cardthartic.com Honoring emotions
- Family search app, Family Tree research
- University of Southern Maine Occupation Therapy
- University of New England Mature Care Medical Group
- National Library of Medicine- NIH
- Roger Lee Miracles Poem
- Paul L. Getter- Solomon's Success Code
- Albert Einstein quotes
- Andy Goldsworthy work

"*Enjoy the little things in life, for one day you may look back and realize they were the big things.*"
—*Robert Bault*

www.ingramcontent.com/pod-product-compliance
Lightning Source LLC
Chambersburg PA
CBHW051007140626
46546CB00016B/1112